Literacy
PRIMER

PETER LANG
New York • Washington, D.C./Baltimore • Bern
Frankfurt am Main • Berlin • Brussels • Vienna • Oxford

Brett Elizabeth Blake
& Robert W. Blake

Literacy
PRIMER

3-20-06

For Preston —
With compliments.

Bob Blake

PETER LANG
New York • Washington, D.C./Baltimore • Bern
Frankfurt am Main • Berlin • Brussels • Vienna • Oxford

Library of Congress Cataloging-in-Publication Data

Blake, Brett Elizabeth.
Literacy primer / Brett Elizabeth Blake, Robert W. Blake.
p. cm.
Includes bibliographical references.
1. Literacy. 2. Sociolinguistics. I. Blake, Robert W. (Robert William). II. Title.
LC149.B53   302.2'244—dc22   2004028055
ISBN 0-8204-7077-5

Bibliographic information published by **Die Deutsche Bibliothek**.
Die Deutsche Bibliothek lists this publication in the "Deutsche
Nationalbibliografie"; detailed bibliographic data is available
on the Internet at http://dnb.ddb.de/.

Cover design by Lisa Barfield

The paper in this book meets the guidelines for permanence and durability
of the Committee on Production Guidelines for Book Longevity
of the Council of Library Resources.

Table of Contents

Introduction

Rationales, Definitions, and New Directions

literacy

The contemporary meaning is simply the ability to read and write. There are at least three levels of literacy: (1) basic literacy; (2) required literacy, and (3) a literacy ranking required for any given social context.

When the word **literacy** *is invoked, strong emotions are often evidenced. People the world over seem to care, sometimes passionately, about people's access to literacy. But literacy is a word with many different definitions and meanings. Indeed, scholars and specialists have failed to agree on what counts as literacy or on its implications. . . . [L]iteracy is quite often associated with the most positive aspects of civilization—such as the graphical image often used in literacy work of a lightbulb turning on with the acquisition of literacy in a person. Yet, literacy encompasses a wide variety of attitudes, beliefs, and power relations between individuals and groups of individuals. The language and scripts of literacy have often been part of human conflicts—intellectual as well as military, social, and cultural change across literate human history. Whether in the efforts of one religious tradition to dominate another or in revolutionary times for one political group to use literacy to break the mold with a past regime, literacy has at times been used or invoked as a way to divide, separate, and rule from a position of power. Literate traditions have also brought diverse ethnic groups together in common pursuits for mutual benefit. Thus, like all human endeavors, literacy often mirrors what is best (and worst) in human history.*

(Wagner, 1999, 1)

The goal of worldwide literacy is probably the most important struggle we face today. We know that people who cannot read and write may be intelligent and worthy persons, but if they are not literate in our

present-day, highly technological, increasingly globalized society, they are at a dismaying disadvantage.

How do we approach the overwhelmingly complex dilemma of worldwide literacy? If we are to improve literacy—even in our country, which enjoys a fairly high literacy rate among citizens—we need to address these questions. What precisely is literacy? If it is fundamentally reading and only secondarily writing, how do we measure the knowledge and skills needed to perform these activities once we have identified and described them? And how do we address contemporary difficulties when we attempt to teach children and adults to read and write? Should we use the precise terms **literate** and **illiterate** to label people, or should we use words placed on a scale, from least important to most crucial, to designate stages of literacy? Is there a single **autonomous literacy**—appropriate for all, such as "standard English" in our country—or are there many different but valuable literacies? And should we provide widespread, but short-range, low-cost "quantity" literacy programs, which from the evidence, we know are minimally successful, or should we concentrate our efforts on long-range, informed, strenuous, and expensive programs, which, on the other hand, have lasting, positive effects?

In a highly developed country with a compulsory universal education tradition, we find it hard to understand countries with no education programs, especially for women. In Marar-I-Sharif, Afghanistan, for instance, we learn that literacy classes for adult women—whose illiteracy rate is estimated to be 85 percent—are forming faster than the government can register them. In the classes presently held in mud-brick neighborhood houses with makeshift blackboards, adult women, sitting on dirt floors, recite the Afghan alphabet as many students nurse babies and others shepherd active toddlers. (Gall, 2002, 1)

"Blind" is the word some of the illiterate women use to describe themselves. Said Torpikay, a thirty-year-old Afghan woman and a student in one of the classes, says, "Without knowledge I am blind. I do not

---

literate

The contemporary meaning of literate relates to the basic ability to read and write at a functional level rather than at a highly developed level.

---

illiterate

A term is reserved for those totally lacking in the ability to read and write and for persons with no or little education.

---

autonomous literacy

The notion of a single benchmark of literacy, unrelated to any social context, such as standard English.

know white from black. In town I do not know where is the hospital, or the baths or the washroom. . . ." Another woman, forty-five-year-old Mahgul, a widow with six children, gives this primal reason for wanting to become literate: "I wanted to know something and help my children. I have no knowledge and so am not a useful person. If I can get some knowledge I can help my children more" (Gall, 2002, 1).

These women understand quite well the consequences of not being able to read and write. Not only do they feel powerless to help their children, but they also can't make out street names or tell the difference between government money and worthless, locally printed bills. Young, illiterate women without husbands or families can't find work, and many report they can't read letters from loved ones who have fled to the mountains or out of the country after years of armed conflict.

In September of 2002, literacy programs administrated by the aid organization, UN–Habitat, already had 172 registered adult classes and reported that new classes were forming faster than the government could accommodate them. The classes for the very few women in Afghanistan who have had some education and may go on to higher learning—in areas where the harshly restrictive influences of the Taliban no longer have a grip—are slim. In former Taliban-ruled areas, girls under eight years of age had been forbidden to attend school. In the Northern Alliance territory in 2001, a mere eight young women were allowed to enroll for the first time in the university with around 300 male students.

At the Gulbahar Orthopedic Center, a male reporter—under the watchful eye of the Center's deputy director—interviews a thirty-year-old midwife, Mazari. She is the first woman in her family to attend a university and now travels from a small town to study at the university in Kabul. What is her urge to become educated? "I wanted to help my people. I wanted to help women," she said.

In the anti-Taliban Alliance territory, girls are allowed to go to all-girl high schools, and a few

lucky young women may attend the university but are permitted to study only a small number of select disciplines, such as medicine, law, and engineering. Said Mazari, "We have freedom. We can shop. We can go to schools. We can teach girls" (Rohde, 2001, B6).

Another woman, a twenty-five-year-old illiterate cleaning woman in the hospital, however, has few such opportunities. Her husband, killed fighting the Taliban, left her with three children to support on a $35-a-month salary. She dreams of becoming a physician, a wish unlikely to come true since she cannot read or write and local customs prevent her from remarrying.

If such stories about illiteracy in Afghanistan sound unbelievably harsh, we have only to turn to India to find conditions disgracefully much the same. One woman, twenty-nine-year-old Kasturi Devi, stands as an example of how literacy programs are changing the face of rural districts in that largest of democracies with a population of over a billion people (Schemetzer, 2000, 14A).

Devi remembers the milestone in her life when she could actually read the sign in her dilapidated bus, announcing "Dholpur," the name of her district capital. When this epiphany occurred, she pushed back the veil covering her head and literally and symbolically revealed her face to the world. On that day, she says she became confident enough to address people as her equal.

In Devi's village, Barehmora, with a population of some 1,000 souls, it is estimated that one third of the inhabitants are literate, but of those only 15 percent are women. Just a few miles away in other villages, we are told, the literacy rate may be zero.

What are the results of becoming literate for the women in these small, rural Indian villages? These are some of the changes in their lives, and in the lives of their families: The women now give the same food to girls as well as to boys, who were previously pampered because they were male. They can now read labels on food cans. They can no longer be cheated by grocers. They now handle finances so their husbands can't stay out, get drunk, and squander the family money. They can decide to have families of no more than two or three children. They can do simple arithmetic, once a male prerogative. They can find jobs or start their own businesses. They are no longer "thumb-stampers," the term for illiterates who use a thumbprint for legal documents because they cannot even sign their names.

The Non-Formal Education Program, partly funded by the World Bank, the European Union, and the Rajiv Gandhi Foundation, is responsible for setting up some 25,000 village schools, which are often housed in mud-brick dwellings with dirt floors (Schemetzer, 2000, 14A).

Even some Indian men are impressed by the advances made by these modestly literate Indian women. One enlightened farmer from Shalekapura, thirty-six-year-old Ram Dhan, remarks as he watches his four daughters attend a class: "I'm not stupid," exemplifying the adage that "I may be dumb, but I'm not stupid." "My girls are educated. They will be valuable wives because they can find a job and earn money for their husbands. I'm sure their husbands will not ask for a dowry [the cost of which frequently bankrupts Indian families]. Perhaps they will pay me."

Not only is there a movement to teach illiterate adult women to read and write in India, but there is also a revolution occurring in elementary school literacy education at the same time in that country (Waldman, 2003, A1, A5). Parents are turning away from the shameful government public schools and enrolling their children in private schools.

Poor, lower-class, illiterate parents who desperately wish their children to become literate are paying cripplingly heavy sums to send their children to newly opened private schools—called "public" schools in the British tradition—particularly if the language of instruction is English. Ram Babu Rai, who as a farmer earns about 1,000 rupees a month ($22), sends one of his three sons to a private school, the

cost of which is 2,200 rupees a year ($49) and includes tuition and the boy's uniform.

It's no wonder children are flocking to private English-language elementary schools. By any account the government schools range from inadequate to disgraceful. It's estimated that 23.8 million children don't even go to school. When they do attend government schools, they sit on dirt floors in buildings with no blackboards, no power, no working latrines, and with either cursory or no teaching going on. In virtually all the government schools in the north of India, the teaching is in Hindi or in one of the regional languages. As a result, parents have been moving their children to private English-speaking schools at a remarkable rate. For such parents, it is apparent they understand well the value of literacy education—in English—as the only hope for social mobility of their children in an increasingly globalized world.

If we believe such depressing examples of illiteracy and the consequences for peoples throughout the world—especially for women—in underdeveloped countries like Afghanistan and India, we may be surprised to discover the problems of literacy here in the United States. For example, we learn of the effects of illiteracy on people living in rural Kentucky. In 2000, a mother of four, the daughter of a coal miner, is, according to statisticians, "functionally illiterate." "With the national economy bubbling along, soaking up workers and spreading wealth, she and much of Appalachia live not only in poverty and unemployment but also with the humiliation of being taken for ignorant"(Kilborn, 2000, A1).

At this point in time, the operational definition for "functionally illiterate" persons is as follows: They are able to read a recipe, follow a map, and work the keys of a McDonald's cash register. On the other hand, they have trouble filling out a job application, typing data into a computer, using standard punctuation in a paragraph, getting their checkbooks to balance, or taking a written test for a driver's license. It is no wonder that such individuals believe themselves to be inferior to those who can read, write, and do simple mathematics in a seemingly effortless manner.

The problem with those labeled "functionally illiterate" is one not only for people isolated in rural Appalachia. According to a survey conducted several years ago by the Educational Testing Service (ETS) for the United States Department of Education, "more than 1 in 5 adults 16 and older, 40 million people in the United States, could read and calculate at no better than the lowest levels of literacy, called Level 1" (Kilborn, 2000, A16). Of these 40 million people, about a quarter are non-English-speaking immigrants while the rest are native speakers of English. Many of those at the Level 1 of literacy are African Americans living in large cities and rural Southern communities. But several million who are considered functionally illiterate are whites living in Appalachia. This national survey and another one conducted recently found that approximately "30 percent of the adults in Appalachia were functionally illiterate" (Kilborn, 2000, A16).

The problem of literacy is not only a challenge for the United States, but is also a difficulty for all other industrialized nations of the world and even more of a problem for developing countries. "Adult literacy statistics both in developing or industrialized countries remain shocking as we approach the end of the twentieth century" (Wagner, 1999, 5). According to Daniel Wagner, UNESCO estimates are that there are still about one billion adult illiterates in the world today, most of whom are to be found in the world's poorest countries.

Reasons for Literacy

Over the centuries, there have been many reasons for establishing and encouraging literacy. The following are the most noteworthy.

Literacy Is Good for the Individual. As Wagner observes: "Literacy is often understood as something that is 'good' for the individual and society" (Wagner,

1999, 2). Although virtually no one believes there should be less literacy, there is widespread disagreement about the meaning of "increased literacy." Notwithstanding the various positions, there appears to be little disagreement about the fact that primary education is one of the chief educational goals of all nations. Even so, nonformal education (NFE) for children and methods for ensuring adult literacy vary a great deal from nation to nation.

The ideal of universal literacy has been articulated by governmental agencies throughout the world. In 1990, at the World Conference on Education for All (WCEFA; UNESCO, 1990), there was general agreement that there should be "literacy for all," as stated in a 1990 declaration (Wagner, 1999, 2). In spite of this consensus, there has, however, been extended debate among countries about how this universal literacy for all individuals is to be achieved.

Literacy Is Good for Economic Well-Being. About the relation of literacy to economic progress, there is little disagreement. Very few countries are unaware that in order to become prosperous, the people of that country must become literate and skilled. The direct cost of illiteracy to the Unites States, for example, has been estimated to be approximately $40 billion a year (Wagner, 1999, 2).

Literacy Is Good for Society. Literacy has important social consequences, especially for women. The majority of illiterate or minimally literate adults, as we have previously discussed, tend to be females, particularly in developing countries, with a surprising amount of correlation established by empirical studies between a lack of literacy and infant mortality and even of the fertility of mothers (Wagner, 1999, 3). We are only now beginning to understand how a mother's lack of education affects her children in many harmful ways. The social consequences of a deficient education or the absence of

literacy schooling appear much more damaging for women than for men.

Literacy Is Good for Political Stability. There has been a long tradition of using language to unify the people of a country. One of the earliest examples was the campaign in Sweden in the 1500s to promote literacy for all citizens, the primary goal being to spread a state religion through Bible study. Although the most important aim was to enable citizens to read Scripture and thus achieve religious solidarity, a secondary aim was to employ literacy as a means of creating a unified nation. More modern examples include movements in Canada, where French-speaking people wish to make French the official language in the province of Quebec; the literacy work in China, Cuba, and the former USSR; as well as the efforts toward literacy in Europe, parts of Asia, and in Africa. In the United States, speakers of Spanish insist that signs in Spanish appear alongside those in English, and the same Spanish speakers are outraged by efforts to have English named the official language of the nation.

The reasons given for establishing a language as the official one of a country include the goals of achieving national solidarity, of lowering social welfare costs, and of providing greater economic productivity. In spite of these claims, most often by those who already speak the target language, there are expected outcries by those who speak a minority language, such as Spanish in the United States. Millions of people deeply resent the imposition of a foreign language—in this case English—and the loss of their native language, representing for them an entire culture.

Literacy Is Good for the Community. There are strong pressures at the grassroots level—from churches, mosques, and other groups at the private, voluntary level—to provide literacy programs, mostly for adults. Such small-scale programs are targeted

at particular groups within the community: out-of-school adolescents, young mothers, the elderly, and the homeless. The government usually has no involvement in these community programs, in which most of the instruction is delivered by volunteer teachers and tutors.

The reason given for such modest programs is that local literacy promotes moral and social cohesion, thus providing a sense of community. We usually find these local programs in industrialized countries, in which the common governmental position is that illiteracy is so marginal that the government need not pay much attention nor provide generous financial support.

Literacy Is Good for Economic Development of Countries. Since the establishment of agencies sponsored by the United Nations after World War II, there have been growing pressures on developing nations to improve their literacy programs. These external pressures are of two kinds.

First, lending agencies such as the World Bank tend to offer loans only if certain types of educational initiatives are promoted and literacy targets are met. At the same time, other UN agencies such as the **United Nations Educational, Scientific, and Cultural Organization (UNESCO)** and the **United Nations Children's Fund (UNICEF)** have supplied considerable financial support for literacy programs in primary schools and for nonformal adult education programs (Wagner, 1999, 4).

Second, certain countries wishing to be perceived as "progressive"—termed the "public appearance" notion—have promoted their efforts at literacy as a way of gaining international and national legitimacy in terms of social progress. Some developing countries, such as Zimbabwe, Tanzania, and Cuba, have advertised their literacy programs in order to gain international recognition as "progressive" countries. Sweden currently publicizes its literacy efforts in terms of social welfare and educational benefits (Wagner, 1999, 4).

UNESCO
The acronym for the United Nations Educational, Scientific, and Cultural Organization.

UNICEF
The acronym for the United Nations Children's Fund, formerly the United Nations International Children's Emergency Fund.

How We Define Literacy

If we search for a single definition upon which most of us can agree, we will be disappointed. It would be useful if standard definitions were set, which would then serve as the basis for policy decisions. There are, however, no precise, neutral definitions for literacy that we all can accept without debate and that will help us in the search for practical means for ensuring universal literacy.

The simplest and most straightforward definition of literacy—and, at the same time, the one that prompts the most discussion—is that "Literacy is the ability to read and write" (Goody, 1999, 29).

Unfortunately, the term 'illiteracy' is commonly associated with poverty and ignorance, for people who are supposedly of below average intelligence or who are "underprivileged." Although large numbers of people who cannot read or write and who live in poverty may be disadvantaged and may indeed be illiterate, we need to emphasize that these individuals are not somehow less intelligent or less worthy as human beings than those who are able to read and write.

As the classicist Eric Havelock argues, the terms "non-literate" or "preliterate" are more acceptable than the disparaging label "illiterate" (Havelock, 1976). He refutes the prevalent myth that non-literate people are barbaric, crude, or primitive, arguing there is irrefutable evidence that from 1100–700 B.C., the ancient Greek culture was made up of totally non-literate, completely oral people who accomplished the most amazing literary, social, cultural, and political feats. They invented the Greek city-state—the *polis*—with all of its essential features in place by the tenth century B.C. During this time non-literate Greeks created a technology for forging iron, thus moving out of the Bronze Age, learned how to navigate ships throughout the Mediterranean and Black Seas, and developed sophisticated modes of commerce. Most significantly, these completely non-literate Greeks fostered the poetic art of the great "singer of tales," Homer, who, most agree, is respon-

sible for creating the enduring oral folk epics the *Iliad* and the *Odyssey*.

In the Greek High Classical Period—the time of Pericles, Sophocles, Euripides, and Aristophanes, and after they had acquired literacy through the invention of alphabetic writing—the Greeks still did not speak of "illiterates" or of "non-literates." In fact, at this time, literacy was not held in high regard; **orality**, not literacy, was the preeminent mode of language. Literacy and cultivation, as considered by most literate people, were not synonymous. The Greeks used the terms "musical," "nonmusical," "educated," and "uneducated," and it wasn't until the fourth century B.C. that the Greeks referred to the *grammatikos* as a "man who could read." "In modern Western society," writes Havelock, "'illiterate' is used to identify that proportion of the population which, because they cannot read or write are presumed to be devoid of intelligence, or else underprivileged. It is therefore pejorative, signifying those who have been left behind in the battle for life, mainly because they are not bright enough" (1976, 3).

Although the term "illiterate" is often used today in a disparaging way, it should be noted that while nonliterate people are still worthwhile despite their lack of literacy, such a term has some merit. If they cannot read, write, and perform basic mathematical functions—we won't even address the matter of "computer literacy" here—nonliterate people may indeed be disadvantaged in our present-day, highly technological society, as well as in the growing number of developing countries in this era of globalization.

orality
The habit of relying entirely on oral communication, rather than on the written word.

Literacy: Many Definitions

The most basic terms "literate" and "illiterate" derive from the Latin *litteratus*, which for Cicero—the Roman statesman, orator, and philosopher who introduced Greek philosophy to Rome—meant a "learned person." In the Middle Ages, a *litteratus* was simply a person who could read Latin. The ability to write was not included in this definition because writing was a completely different matter from the act of reading. Apparently literate people found it difficult—physically as well as mentally—to master the skills of using ink and quills to write on very scarce and precious parchment, a writing surface made from the skins of sheep or goats (Venezky, 1990, 3).

After 1300 A.D. a *litteratus* was a person with a minimal ability to read Latin, mainly because of the breakdown of learning during the Middle Ages. With the spread of vernacular languages after the Reformation—the period during the sixteenth century in which there was an effort to reconstitute Western Christendom—literate persons became those that could both read and write in their native languages.

Although we don't find the word "literacy" in the English lexicon until the end of the nineteenth century, the actual ideas of literate and illiterate date from the last half of the sixteenth century. The classical definition of literacy survived until at least 1740, evidence of which is found in a quote by Lord Chesterfield, as cited in the *Oxford English Dictionary* (OED), in which an "illiterate" is ignorant of Greek and Latin (Venezky, 1990, 3).

When the word "literate" is applied to those with highly developed reading and writing abilities, the adjectives "advanced" or "high" are used. One writer, for instance, identifies those who are "highly literate" as individuals who can read—and, we assume, make sense of—William Faulkner's fiction and of Ludwig Wittgenstein's philosophy (Ashiem, quoted in Venezky, 1990, 3).

"Literate" is used today to refer to lower levels of reading and writing, rather than to an above-average skill level. Another writer, discussing literacy in Anglo-Saxon England, used the terms "pragmatic (practical) literacy," referring to lower levels of literacy, and "cultured literacy" to signify a higher-than-normal level of literacy (Wormwald, quoted in Venezky, 1990, 3).

As a first step in defining "literacy" for modern usage, we employ it to refer to a minimal or near-minimal level of skills, a meaning quite distinct from the use of "literacy" as applied to a high or advanced category. At the same time, we use "literacy" for the ability of an individual to make sense of print in most newspapers—which are commonly rated at the ninth-grade reading level—probably excluding newspapers like the *New York Times,* whose "readability" is at a much higher level. The use of the word "literacy" implies that an individual can show at least a minimal ability to read and write. Even though at one time the term "literacy" was applied to the ability to read only, it probably makes sense now to use "literacy" to mean the ability to read as well as to write.

A problem greater than agreeing on a precise definition of the word "literacy" is arriving at a consensus for a meaning of the word "illiteracy." Those who are labeled 'illiterate' are individuals who fall below some cutoff point, no matter how we define that level. For example, those who are able to read and write very simple prose may frequently be labeled "illiterate" along with those who are not able to read or write at all. In order to create a single definition of "illiteracy" for the purposes of discussion, the term "illiterate" is reserved for "those totally lacking reading/ writing knowledge" (Venezky, 1990, 4).

How We Define Functional Literacy

functional literacy
A term with at least two meanings: (1) a minimal level at which an individual exhibits the ability to read and write a simple prose paragraph; and (2) the ability to use literacy for practical purposes, to get something done.

The next term to be defined is that of **functional literacy**. It is interesting but of little practical value to note all the qualifying terms attached to the idea of functional literacy: "conventional literacy," "survival literacy," "marginal literacy," and "functional adult literacy." Most writers, however, use the term "functional literacy" according to the definition first used by UNESCO in the 1950s. "In several seminal studies done by that agency, literacy was viewed as a continuum of skills, including both reading and writing" (Venezky, 1990, 4). By this definition, literacy means "procedural knowledge,"

or the ability to "do" something. This is in opposition to "declarative knowledge"—having knowledge "about" something. Such a distinction is analogous to being able to write an essay in opposition to being able to repeat definitions related to expository writing, like the terms "thesis" and "supporting details"—knowing about writing. In the late 1950s, UNESCO proposed that the concept of literacy be divided into two levels: a minimal level, in which an individual demonstrates the ability to read and write a simple prose message, and a functional level, in which a person achieves a level of literacy high enough to function in a social setting.

Age and Functional Literacy

A crucial element in an adequate definition of functional literacy is one's performance in society. When we think about this feature, it is necessary to relate functional literacy to the ages of individuals. If functional literacy means success in various situations, individuals cannot be held accountable until they are able to practice these skills, at least until they near adulthood.

When we examine the practices of a number of social agencies in reporting functional literacy, we learn that young children are not held responsible for literacy skills. The U.S. Census Bureau, for instance, when it dealt with literacy statutes from 1870 through 1930, reported the results for children only two years of age or older, while from 1959 to 1969, the statistics were reported only for individuals fourteen and older (Venezky, 1990, 5). In addition, the Division of Adult Basic Education of the U.S. Office of Education included in its data statistics only for individuals sixteen years and older. And finally, the UNESCO Expert Committee on Standardization of Educational Statistics recommended that reports on literacy should deal with persons of the minimum age of fifteen years or older. If we think about the matter of age as related to literacy—and the term "literacy" meaning the ability to read and write—it is

ridiculous to designate a five-year-old who could not read and write as "illiterate."

So how do we arrive at an age—as arbitrary as the designated limit may be—when individuals may be identified as being able to use literacy skills to function in society, at work, for home management, and for voting intelligently? Teenagers in most of the United States cannot receive work permits until they reach the age of sixteen, and they cannot vote until they are eighteen. When we use age as a criterion for identifying levels of literacy, we fail to take into account the exceptions to an age-level limit; the idea of an "age range" at which a person may use literacy skills makes more sense. What is more significant than a person's arbitrary age is his or her ability to use literacy in the following ways: to drive responsibly, to be successful in the workplace, to be conscious of local, regional, national, and global politics and economics, to take part in social and recreational activities, and to make decisions about what educational paths to follow. "It seems reasonable to continue to use literacy as a referent for adult or near-adult abilities and to avoid such compounds as "functional adult literacy" and "functional child literacy" (Venezky, 1990, 6). We are, therefore, on firm ground when we use the term "functional literacy"to mean an acceptable grasp of the skills of reading and writing for functioning in society as a young adult.

Literacy Skills

If we accept the phrase "functional literacy" to refer to a minimal level of literacy and view "literacy" as an overall term for a set of higher literacy skills, what are the necessary skills in these categories? One scheme for defining these skills can be found in research done by the National Assessment of Educational Progress (NAEP) Adult Work Skills and Knowledge Assessment, done in 1973–1974, and from the Adult Performance Level Functional Literacy Test, also developed in the 1970s: literacy skills for occupational, civic, community, and personal functioning (Venezky, 1990, 7). In other surveys, these broad categories of literacy skills are usually included: reading, writing, numeracy, and document processing. Though the skill of reading is present in all surveys, there continues to be widespread disagreement on the levels or types of reading necessary for functional literacy. To assess literacy skills in schools, tests usually include reading exposition and fiction selections with multiple-choice questions that measure vocabulary levels and expository and literary comprehension. Even though the test results are reported for grade levels, most experts maintain grade-level scores tell us little about the literacy of adults and offer little information about the wide range of literacy abilities for school children at various grade levels.

With respect to writing, there is not yet enough empirical evidence about the skills for writing to set criteria levels for writing literacy. "We are, however, far from developmental norms for composition, in spite of expanded research and assessment activities" (Venezky, 1990, 8). Although a great deal of effort has been expended since 1990, we are still far from agreeing on the skills necessary for effective writing ability at different age levels.

Most knowledgeable persons include numeracy in the broad skills of overall literacy, but again, as we might suspect, there is little agreement on what precisely is meant by **numerate literacy**. One reason for establishing numerate literacy is that any skills beyond simple addition and subtraction are too difficult to include in a definition of basic numeracy. As the arguments goes if we include higher skills such as multiplication and division—not to say the competency skills of algebra, trigonometry, and calculus—we leave out a sizable population from the ranks of those who are numerately literate.

In order to decide what numeracy skills should be included, we must await in-depth analyses of the skills necessary for functioning in a highly technological society. Rather, we might better "confine functional literacy to those numeric operations that are critical for an ordinary meaning of print: basic

numerate literacy

The ability to think and express oneself with numbers, or the skills critical for ordinary meaning in print, such as basic addition, comparison (greater than, less than), dates, and times.

addition and subtraction, comparisons (greater than, less than), dates, times, and perhaps a few others" (Venezky, 1990, 5). Such an array of numeracy skills is indeed minimal for our modern society.

The fourth major category within functional literacy is document knowledge, and as we might anticipate, this group of skills is also difficult to define precisely because of the lack of systematic inquiry into the matter. Document knowledge is generally defined as consisting of "the ability to make sense of documents such as these: tax schedules (which are becoming more and more complex), television schedules, advertisements, and labels on products" (Venezky, 1990, 9). It is not enough, however, to simply list the various types of documents persons must "read" and make sense of. What is critically needed, however, is that we somehow identify the skills used in document processing and describe in detail the psychological demands required of individuals who successfully negotiate various kinds of documents from the simplest to the most complex—like a modern tax form.

In summary, however we describe the broad categories of functional literacy, we are left with an obvious conclusion: the ability to read is the overarching skill of literacy. Although writing, numeracy, and document processing are important elements of functional literacy, each of these skills is highly dependent upon reading ability. If by functional writing we mean making shopping lists, writing down messages, and then making notes on what has been read, then writing becomes a "craft" skill—such as that performed by medieval scribes—that of merely copying words. At the same time, persons who cannot read will obviously perform numerate skills "in their heads" or "on their fingers" and will only be able to react orally to documents read to them. If they cannot read, then, persons who are unable to perform basic math skills or fill out documents are severely disadvantaged in our society. On the one hand, persons who can read at a basic level—and who can use a modern calculator and computer—but who possess low-level numeracy skill, may be able to function quite respectably. On the other hand, those persons who are skilled in arithmetic and in working their way through documents—usually with the help of individuals who are able to read at least on a functional level—and who are intelligent, hardworking, and highly motivated will be frustrated with their lack of opportunities to succeed in a society increasingly dependent upon people with advanced literacy skills.

Critical Levels of Literacy

We are aware that literacy abilities for persons in our society may range from those who are unable to read or write to those whose literacy skills go right off any scale used to measure reading and writing. How then to measure minimal literacy? We may take the recommendation made by UNESCO in 1957 to report two levels of literacy: minimal literacy and functional literacy.

With respect to literacy for reading, we now have evidence of the complex of skills necessary for effective reading, particularly of alphabetic script and print systems. On the basis of an analysis of the common core of psychological abilities necessary for reading, we are thus able to identify the crucial abilities essential for reading. We can have children learn and practice these core reading skills, and then assess how well children may perform these skills and as a result have proof of their ability to read. Such skills include recognizing instantaneously the relationship between the sounds of speech and the written symbols used to represent them and then to move from comprehending syllables to single words to groups of words in longer and more complex phrases and clauses. Finally, neophyte readers need to learn such skills as making sense of unfamiliar words by context and by deferring comprehension until a good deal of material has been read.

Over the last several decades, there has been much research, observation, analysis, and speculation dealing with the writing process and the teach-

ing of writing. From this significant body of information, we are now in a much better position to name and describe the required skills for writing, from writing simple messages to writing expository prose and responding in writing to literature. As a result of this increased knowledge about how to teach writing, most experts term the approach "process writing," by which one follows a series of at least four recursive stages: prewriting, first-draft writing, revising, and editing. As we are presently able to devise realistic criteria for measuring reading skills, we are now able to assess writing skills essential for effective and worthwhile writing.

If we are able to define the skills vital for achieving numerate literacy and **document literacy**—and it seems evident that computer literacy may be added to the preceding elements of literacy—then we may define the following levels of literacy: "'basic literacy,' which denotes the level that allows self-sustained development in literacy; 'required literacy,' which applies to a level that allows self-sustained, independent development in literacy; and 'advanced literacy,' which is the literacy ranking required for any given social context and which might, therefore, change over time, place social condition" (Venezky, 1990, 11).

It is important to note that serious students of literacy will not accept grade-level equivalents as proof of literacy levels. One drawback to applying grade-level performance to literacy levels is the fact that, although writing skills—including the writing of whole essays as well as responding to multiple-choice items about writing—are not a staple of most literacy instruments, reading is still the primary activity for measuring literacy. There remains much work to be done to determine what exactly we shall label as numeracy, document processing, and, it appears inevitable, computer literacy.

The other major drawback to using grade levels for justifying literacy levels is that grade levels are arrived at from what the majority of school- aged children can do at certain grade levels and therefore are

document literacy

The capacity to make sense of documents, such as tax forms, television schedules, advertisements, and product labels.

not appropriate for measuring adult literacy. For instance, research has shown—and it is only common sense to recognize this—that we read more easily and with better comprehension subject matter about which we already know a great deal. Adults, because of their life experiences, may be much more successful at reading a particular text than a child reading the same text, who has had little or no experience with the subject.

Related to the skill of reading material of a familiar nature is the problem of reading various kinds of printed texts. Some persons, who are accustomed to reading exposition, may read expository essays and books with ease, but, who, because they may have had little experience with reading literature, may have considerable trouble in reading fiction, poetry, and especially plays. Even though school tests of literacy frequently include questions dealing with fiction and poetry, virtually none of the discussions of literacy include the skills of reading literature. It's almost as if there is an assumption in our culture that reading literature is not really important if one wishes to become literate, that reading literature is an unnecessary frill for a literate person. With the advent of a recent movement called **Classroom Reader Response**, we may come to recognize that reading literature, although it employs a set of skills radically different from reading exposition, is a unique way of knowing and an integral element of literacy (Blake, 1996)

Classroom Reader Response

An approach to reading literature where the emphasis is on the individual reader's emotional and intellectual response—as a result of the person's age, gender, race, cultural background, and so forth—to the literary work.

New Literacy Demands

If we are concerned with the level of functional literacy skills for those in our workforce, we recognize that the literacy demands have changed drastically over the centuries and, of course, have changed at a dizzying pace over the last several decades. Some maintain that the complexity of grammar and the difficulty of vocabulary may not have changed from the nineteenth century for legal documents, newspapers, and public announcements and that they may have even become simpler than

they were 100 years ago. Though the complexity of functional reading material may not have changed, the sheer quantity of print has increased. As a result, we all have to read more material and read it faster than we once did.

Another problem with new literacy claims relates literacy to the changing labor demands in our rapidly expanding technological society rather than to concerns about manufacturing positions. Literacy requirements for workers in the future will alter in ways we find difficult to anticipate. In any event, we need to be aware of contemporary employment requirements and resulting alterations in our notions about literacy and to make the necessary adjustments for teaching reading and writing and assessing these literacy skills. "Perhaps we need a literacy index, equivalent to the consumer price index, to register yearly shifts in functional literacy requirements. With or without such codification of change, an adequate definition of literacy must incorporate changing literacy demands in some meaningful way" (Venezky, 1990, 13).

Future Directions in Literacy Study

The future of literacy depends on the ability of researchers, teachers, and policy makers to come to agreement not only on definitions of literacy but also about descriptions of the elements of reading and writing, as well as the standards required for literacy in at least these major areas. What follow are some of the concerns we now have for the future of literacy study throughout the world.

Literacy/ Illiteracy Versus a Scale of Literacy Skills. Before World War II, it was common to make a distinction between those who had some schooling and those who hadn't as a basis for measuring literacy. This was particularly true in developing countries. At the beginning of the twenty-first century, this situation has changed dramatically. Although there are still millions who have had no schooling, even in the poorest countries most of the youngest generations are usually reported as having some formal education. In the light of this situation, it would seem that a more finely tuned method of measuring degrees of literacy than simply "schooled" or "not schooled" is needed.

One remaining difficulty with a more accurate method for measuring literacy is the evidence that many countries continue to report on literacy using the "literate/ illiterate" distinction. As a result, such statistics from these countries are grossly inaccurate and therefore virtually meaningless. "Learning Achievement" instruments would provide much more sophisticated ways of measuring actual literacy. Wagner defines the issue in this way: "The point here is the previous dichotomy is not only inaccurate and of little use today but is also misleading in terms of the types of policies that need to be put into place. Yet it is a dichotomy that is dying a relatively slow death, though it seems likely that this situation will change as we move toward 2000" (Wagner, 1999, 5).

A Single Literacy Versus Many Literacies. One aspect of the debate over a single literacy versus many literacies involves the tendency of some to list "literacies" other than reading and writing, such as computer literacy, geographical literacy, historical literacy, scientific literacy, and even what is called design literacy. Since it is the responsibility of the varied disciplines involved to define their respective "literacies," we believe it is our obligation here to deal with "literacy" only as it relates to reading and writing.

The notion of a single literacy, a set of global skills related to reading and writing, unrelated to any social context, is known as the "autonomous" model of literacy. As sociologist Brian Street defines this literacy, "It is treated as 'autonomous' in the sense that it has its own characteristics, irrespective of time and place in which it occurs and also in the sense

that it has consequences for society that can be derived from its distinctive and intrinsic character" (1999, 35).

The person most closely associated with the idea of a single, autonomous literacy, Jack Goody, argues that a single literacy was responsible for the shift from preliterate to literate cultures and thus was responsible for the development of modern Western society. Writing, according to this thesis, as the foundation of modern literacy "fosters and 'enforces' the invention of formal logic, the study of history instead of myth, the growth of governmental bureaucracies, the shift from small villages to much larger cities, the beginnings of modern science (because observations and findings can now be published), and even the birth of democratic political processes and institutions . . . we can be detached, critical, reflective only because writing allows us to express ourselves outside the constraints of ordinary every day intercourse" (Goody, quoted in Street, 1999, 35).

Though other scholars have argued against the position that the distinction between oral discourse and literacy is overstated, Goody extends his debate about the autonomous nature of literacy to law, bureaucratic organizations, and even to economic development. With the advent of literacy, he notes, courts relied on the written word rather than on notoriously unreliable oral testimony. Writing also promotes the autonomy of bureaucracies, since writing allows organizations to keep written records in order to develop a body of procedures (e.g., the Constitution of the United States, Constitutional Amendments, and Supreme Court decisions), and to educate those who specialize in creating and maintaining organizations. With respect to the effect of literacy on the development of Third World countries, Goody believes "a certain rate of literacy is often seen as necessary to radical change, partly from the limited standpoint of being able to read the instructions on the seed packet, partly because of the increased autonomy even with regard to the seed packet of the autodidact" (Goody, 1986, 45).

Other writers have attempted to modify Goody's position. Olson, for one, has softened his own earlier attitude that literacy is indeed autonomous. However, rather than stating that there is a single, autonomous model of literacy for all peoples throughout the world, Olson now argues that literacy, by bringing language into our consciousness, not only aids our memory but on a deeper level changes how we know and thus is culturally determined. "The differences between speech and writing and the complex relations between them make writing a powerful tool of cognition, a tool central to cultural development in the West and elsewhere as well" (Olson, 1999, 132). In effect, literacy changes the way we think, believes Olson, and it "gives us the ability to step into, and on occasion to step out again, from this new world, the world on paper" (Olson, 1994, 18).

The idea of "many literacies" is most prominently advanced by Brian Street, who has labeled this idea "social literacies" (Street, 1995a). For Street, it is obvious that literacy is always practiced in social situations. What is not so apparent is that this truism has important ramifications for accepted definitions of literacy as well as implications for how literacy is then taught and learned. Expanding on the topic of "social literacies," and "literacy practices," some scholars now speak of **multiple literacies**—such as "community literacies," "local literacies," and "individual literacies."

Even within a given culture, so this argument goes, there are numerous literacies, including all examples of reading and writing inside formal educational institutions as well as beyond school walls. Street explains the idea of "literacy practices" in this way: "From this perspective one may ask what are the literacy practices at home of children whose schooled practices are judged problematic or idiomatic. From the school's point of view, those home practices may represent simply inferior attempts at the real thing; from the researcher's point of view these home practices represent as important a part of the repertoire

multiple literacies
The notion that there are numerous appropriate and therefore acceptable literacies practiced in any number of social situations, including those used at home and in other environments, as well as a distinctive literacy traditionally employed in schools.

as different languages or language varieties" (Street, 1999, 38).

Quantity Literacy Education Versus Quality Literacy Education. This problem is especially troublesome for literacy education, particularly for adult literacy education, relating directly to the definition of the term "literate." When does an "illiterate" person become "literate"? If it is a simple matter to make a person "literate," then campaigns such as "Literacy Volunteers" or literacy teachers' corps should be successful. Volunteers don't need long periods of training, the periods of instruction for students need not be extensive, and therefore highly advertised, popular programs of instruction are quick and cheap ways to make large numbers of individuals literate.

Research reveals, unfortunately, that such programs don't deliver as much as their advocates promise. Volunteers seldom stay long enough to become accomplished teachers, and choices about what language is to be the target language are usually decided on a political basis rather than by careful study of which language—such as French or English in Quebec—would be most desirable for those people living in a particular county, state, or country (Wagner, 1999, 6).

Summary

1   **Illiterate People Are Still Worthy Individuals.** Although people who are not literate are worthwhile and may have achieved magnificent cultures, in the present era of increasing technology and globalization, people who cannot read or write are simply at a disadvantage in life.
2   **Reasons for People to Become Literate.** The major reasons for persons to become literate are individual (personal development and fulfillment), economic, social, and political.
3   **Conflicting Terms for Literacy.** As a sign of the chaotic nature of the study of literacy, definitions

such as "pre-literate," "non-literate," "highly literate," and "marginally literate" abound. The most commonly used definitions are "literate," "illiterate," and "functionally literate," although the range of meanings applied to these terms is enormously wide.

4 **Problems to Be Dealt With in the Future.** The most pressing problems are the following: (1) Literacy versus Illiteracy; (2) A Single Literacy versus Many Literacies; and (3) Quality versus Quantity Literacy Education.

5 **New Directions for Literacy Investigation.** These are some possible future directions for literacy investigation:

—We need to move away from the simplistic distinctions between "literacy" and "illiteracy," from the idea that the problem of literacy is a simple one, that literacy is like a "lightbulb," which "simply needs to be turned on" to make a person literate, or that literacy is merely a matter of political will.

—We need to recognize that there is not one "literacy" for all occasions, that literacy is a human rights issue, an educational right, and at the same time, a legitimate aspect of national and global efforts to improve education, individual development, well-being, and self-respect. In spite of the widespread notion that literacy may be relatively easy to accomplish, serious students of literacy now realize that literacy is a much more complex matter than first was believed, even when we agree—which we seldom do—on what literacy is.

—As a sign of the increased interest in all aspects of literacy, researchers from many fields, including history, linguistics, psycholinguistics, sociolinguistics, and education, are making significant contributions to our understanding of literacy. As a result, we may see the development of accurate indices of literacy, a new foundation for literacy research, and recently and soon-to-be discovered methods for teaching all

aspects of literacy—based upon research and extensive practical applications of the research related to teaching reading and writing—with all of this progress in the pursuit of an admirable but possibly unattainable goal of universal literacy.

Glossary

autonomous literacy—The notion of a single benchmark of literacy, unrelated to any social context, such as standard English.

Classroom Reader Response—An approach to reading literature where the emphasis is not on the author's original intent or solely on the text itself but rather on the individual reader's emotional and intellectual response—as a result of the person's age, gender, race, cultural background, and so forth—to the literary work.

document literacy—The capacity to make sense of documents, such as tax forms, television schedules, advertisements, and product labels.

functional literacy—A term with at least two meanings: (1) a minimal level at which an individual exhibits the ability to read and write a simple prose paragraph; and (2) the ability to use literacy for practical purposes, to get something done. Note that such definitions omit the skills for reading and writing literary texts.

illiterate—As applied to persons, who, because of a lack of education, cannot read and write and yet are intelligent and worthwhile individuals, the terms "nonliterate" and "preliterate" are preferred. The term "illiterate" was used in eighteenth-century England for those who were ignorant of Latin and Greek. In contemporary usage, the term is reserved for those totally lacking in the ability to read and write and for persons with no or little education.

literacy—The contemporary meaning is simply the ability to read and write. We may, however, think of at least three levels of literacy: (1) basic literacy, a level that allows self-sustained self-development; (2) required literacy, a level that applies to self-sustained, independent development in literacy; and (3) a literacy ranking required for any given social context, which may therefore change over time, place, and social condition. With this definition, no reference is made

to reading and writing literature, the sole reference being to prose literacy.

literate—A term capable of many shades of meaning and one that has changed over the centuries. The ancient Greeks termed an individual who could read only a *grammatikos*. For the Latin orator and philosopher Cicero in the first century B.C. a *litteratus* was a learned person. In the Middle Ages, a *litteratus* was a person who could read Latin. For most of the long history of the word in English, the word "literate" referred to a person knowledgeable about literature and, in a general sense, one who was "well educated," "learned."

The contemporary meaning of literate relates to the basic ability to read and write at a functional level rather than at a highly developed level, such as a person who can make sense of the fiction of William Faulkner or the philosophy of Albert Camus.

In recent times, the terms "literate" and "illiterate" have been expanded from the original reference to reading and literature to numerous bodies of knowledge, such as one being historically literate, computer literate, and even design literate.

multiple literacies—The notion that rather than a single, standard autonomous literacy, there are numerous appropriate and therefore acceptable literacies practiced in any number of social situations, including those used at home and in other environments, as well as a distinctive literacy traditionally employed in schools.

numerate literacy—The ability to think and express oneself with numbers.

At the most basic level, the skills critical for ordinary meaning in print, such as basic addition, comparison (greater than, less than), dates, and times.

orality—The primary meaning of this new term is the habit of relying entirely on oral communication, rather than on the written word. The term was coined deliberately on the analogy of the word "literacy," in order to denote the skill of oral communication in a positive sense and to avoid the implications of failure conveyed by the term "illiteracy."

UNESCO—The acronym for the United Nations Educational, Scientific, and Cultural Organization.

UNICEF—The acronym for the United Nations Children's Fund, formerly the United Nations International Children's Emergency Fund.

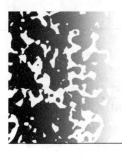

The Foundations of Literacy and Its Consequences

The introduction of the Greek letters into inscription somewhere about 700 B.C. was to alter the character of human culture, placing a gulf between all alphabetic societies and their precursors. The Greeks did not just invent an alphabet; they invented literacy and the literate base of modern thought. Under modern conditions there seems to be only a short time lag between the invention of a device and its full social or industrial application, and we have got used to this idea of a fact of technology. This was not true of the alphabet. The letter shapes and values had to pass through a period of localization before being standardized throughout Greece. Even after the technology was standardized or relatively so—there were always two competing versions, the Eastern and the Western—the effects were registered slowly in Greece, were partly cancelled during the European Middle Ages, and have been fully realized only since the further invention of the printing press.

(Havelock, 1976, 44, 45)

Why should we be concerned with the foundations of literacy? If we can read and write passably well, is that not enough? Should we bother to learn where reading and writing come from? In what ways is writing different from speech? What is the story of the

development over many centuries of reading and writing, and what is the precise nature of the kind of reading and writing we presently use? What are the conditions necessary for large numbers of people—not just an elite—to be able to read and write? How has this radical, technological invention—for reading is a human invention—come literally, in the most amazing way, to change the way we think?

In this chapter, we shall deal with such questions. Most of the time, we do not bother to think much about how we speak, read, and write because such activities come so naturally to most of us that they are usually below the level of our consciousness. As we become more sophisticated in our ability to use language, we may feel the need to adjust our language to differing social situations and for various purposes. In short, we may arrive at an understanding of how reading literally changes the workings of our minds.

Speaking and Writing

Why study speech when our concern is with reading and writing? Because inscribed signs—"inscribed" meaning carved and engraved on clay tablets, stone, and wood, as well as written on animal skins, papyrus, and paper—are attempts to represent objects, ideas, and sounds on relatively permanent surfaces. If we can imagine our world without print, how would we use symbols to show what we see or hear in language? We can draw pictures of things and numbers; for example, we might draw pictures of two cats or a house or a new moon. But how would we show the words "love" or "beauty" or "truth"? And how would we use signs rather than pictures to show ideas or objects?

We have a long history of using writing for many purposes, a history during which we invented several writing systems and eventually arrived at the invention of the alphabetic system of writing.

Characteristics of Speech

trachea	

trachea
Also caled the windpipe. A tube by which air is sent from the lungs through the pharynx, larynx, and the oral or nasal cavities and by which the sounds of language are produced.

glottis
The opening between the vocal cords at the upper part of the larynx, also known as the vocal bands.

unvoiced sound
A sound made with the vocal bands (glottis) open or unobstructed.

resonating cavities
Hollow chambers where speech sounds are created: the pharyngeal cavity (area in back of throat), nasal cavity (nose), and oral cavity (mouth).

pharynx
The section of the alimentary canal that runs from the mouth and nasal cavities to the larynx.

articulators
Organs of speech that change sounds by moving parts of the mouth, including the lower lip, the tongue, and the uvula (the movable flap in the back of the mouth.)

How is speech different from reading or writing? First of all, we need to accept the fact that speech comes first in language. Human beings, we might say, are biologically—as well as mentally—"programmed" for speech.

No other creature on earth has the physical apparatus for speech, contrary to what is argued for chimpanzees' or gorillas' ability to "speak." We explain the physical process of speaking here because through this knowledge we come to comprehend how speech is physically divided into the sounds we term "consonants" and "vowels." It was the discovery of these speech elements that led to the invention of the alphabet, which in turn provides the foundation for literacy.

How physically do humans make speech? First we send air from our lungs up through the windpipe, or **trachea**. Now how do we turn that column of air into speech? As the air is sent through the windpipe, it meets the **vocal bands**, or **glottis**, which can be open or closed. If the bands are open, we have an **"unvoiced"** sound, such as the first sound in the word "thin." If the vocal bands are constricted, we make a "voiced" noise, such as the initial sound in the word "then."

How else can we alter this column of air into distinctly different sounds? Primarily, we modify the air so that it becomes one of the two fundamental sounds, either a consonant or a vowel. We can do that first through the "**resonating cavities**": the **pharyngeal** *cavity,* the area way in the back of the throat; the *nasal cavity;* and the *oral cavity.* In speech, we change the shape and open or close off these cavities to alter sounds.

Next, we can change sounds by moving parts of the mouth, the "**articulators**": the lower lip, the tongue, and the *uvula,* the little flap that hangs down in the back of the mouth.

Finally, we change the sounds by placing the movable parts against the fixed parts of the mouth, called the "**points of articulation**": the upper lip, the upper teeth, the *alveolar ridge* (the bony ridge toward the front of the roof of the mouth), the *palate* (the soft part of the upper mouth), and the *velum* (the part of the upper mouth in the back).

Now, back to the vibration of air in the throat. After being modified by the vocal bands, the air is then sent past the pharynx and through either the mouth or the nose, where we make one of two choices. If we modify this vibration in some way so that it is "unobstructed," we call that sound a **vowel**. Different vowel sounds are produced by shaping resonating cavities. But if we stop or start the vibrating air in some way by moving the articulators against the points of articulation, the sound produced is called a **consonant**.

"Although both 'vowel' and 'consonant' seek to describe sounds, they were coined only after the Greek alphabet made these sounds 'visually' recognizable as 'letters,' and strictly speaking vowel and consonant, derived from the Latin, denote types of letters of the Greek alphabet" (Havelock, 1976, 29). So, contrary to the belief still held by many that writing is the primary mode of language, speech in fact comes first. The use of scripts is a comparatively late technological invention, alphabetic writing—generally acknowledged as the only genuine writing—being invented around 750 B.C. by the Greeks.

The Development of Writing

Literacy—essentially reading and writing—has spread historically "through communication between people who possessed written languages and those who did not" (Bernard, 1999, 22). People from different cultures came in contact chiefly through trade, religion, and schooling. The contact through schooling generally came about as a dominant people forced their own language upon a conquered people.

Scholars estimate that 3,000 years ago there were some 500,000 bands, tribes, and states—all independent groups of people—who spoke mutually unintelligible languages. Today, we are told, there are people in some 200 countries who speak—and sometimes write—approximately 6,000 different languages. Because of increased methods of communication, these peoples, and therefore their languages, are in contact more than were ancient peoples (Bernard, 1999, 22). The generally accepted view is that people invented writing independently of each other in the New World as well as in Europe and the Middle East. Early writing systems were invented in the Old World in ancient Mesopotamia around 3200 B.C. and spread throughout the region through cultural contact. For example, the writing system first used in the ancient Indus civilization may very well have been spread by traders from the Middle East. Others, who argue that writing originated in Mesopotamia, believe that writing was initially developed in what is now Iraq, Egypt, India, or even as far east as China.

Wherever and whenever a type of writing was first invented in the Old World, there is now general agreement that writing was also invented—without any influence from the Old World—in the New World in what is now Mexico. The Olmecs, according to the evidence of inscriptions, developed a writing system of some 180 glyphs. (A glyph is an inscribed symbolic figure representing a figure or object. The prefix "hiero-" comes from the Greek *hieros,* "sacred," and thus, the word "hieroglyphic," used for Egyptian religious carved symbols, refers to ancient Egyptian sacred writings.) The Olmec system was used throughout parts of present-day Mexico around 600 B.C. It is estimated that there may have been as many as fifteen different writing systems in pre-Columbian Mexico. Unfortunately, the Europeans who arrived in Mexico in the sixteenth century stopped all instruction in the original languages and also destroyed all existing manuscripts. Since 1521, natives in Mexico and throughout Latin

America have continued writing their indigenous languages—not in the original glyphs, however, but in the alphabetic script that the conquerors brought from Europe (Bernard, 1999, 22).

Most scholars break scripts, or writing systems, into roughly three categories.

First, in **logographic scripts**, the earliest scripts, signs and symbols represent entire words, such as the symbol "$" for "dollar" and the letter "e" for "energy" in physics. (The word "logographic" is based on the Greek *logos*, "word," and *graphos*, "written," which, when joined together, means "to write a word.") Each logograph is a single visual sign standing for an individual word. The number of different logographs for the major words in a language, as we might imagine, can be very large. A major drawback with logographic writing is simply memorizing the daunting number of symbols.

Second are **syllabic scripts**. As we can surmise, such scripts use symbols to represent not words but syllables. Such a script generally uses some three hundred signs per language and presents problems not only with memorizing all the syllables but also with remembering which symbol stands for which syllable.

Third are **alphabetic scripts**. Alphabetic scripts, it is argued, are the only full-fledged scripts and provide the most efficient kind of writing. They use symbols to represent the basic elements of speech, its "**phonemes**," the smallest units of meaningful sound in any language. It is important to understand this concept if we are to understand alphabetic writing.

The words "run" and "pun," for instance, begin with different sounds: /r/ and /p/. (The slashes show the representation of phonemes in print, to differentiate them from letters in "conventional orthography," the term for writing in ordinary written language.) These sounds are significantly different for speakers of English—that is, as speakers of English we hear them as different sounds—and therefore they are different phonemes in English. The letter "u" in

---

logographic script

Writing in which a written symbol (logograph or ideograph) stands for an individual word. For instance, the symbol 4 is read as "four" in English and as "quatre" in French.

---

syllabic script

Writing in which symbols represent not sounds (alphabetic script) or words (logographic script) but rather syllables.

---

alphabetic script

Writing or print in which symbols stand for phonemes, the smallest meaningful sounds of a language, rather than symbols representing objects and ideas or syllables.

---

phoneme

The smallest unit of meaningful sound in a language, e.g. the sounds represented by the letter u in "run" and "pun" are identical phonemes. The letters "r" and "p" represent different phonemes. The letter "p" in the words "spin" and "pin," however, represents different sounds (phones), but since the sounds are not meaningfully different, they represent the same phoneme/p/.

the two words represents the same sound and therefore indicates the same phoneme.

But there is more to this business of a phoneme. Consider the words "pin" and "spin." The sound for "p" in the word "pin" is actually different from the sound for "p" in the word "spin." If you don't believe it, try this experiment. While holding a lighted match a few inches from your mouth, repeat the word "spin" several times: "spin, spin, spin." The flame wavers but does not go out. Now say "pin, pin, pin." With the first "pin," the flame is extinguished. The "p" in "pin" is pronounced with a slight puff of air. Although the sound for "p" in "pin" and the sound for the "p" in "spin" are *acoustically* different, they are not different in a meaningful way to a speaker of English. We interpret them as the same sound. Both sounds, therefore, are represented as the same phoneme in English: /p/.

There is no difference, though, in sound between the two initial written symbols in the words "cite" and "sight," although the written letters are different. Thus, though there is a written difference—a "**graphemic**" difference—between the two letters, there is no phonemic difference between the sounds represented, in this case, by the letters "c" and "s."

If the alphabetic script invented by the Greeks in the eighth century B.C. is the only authentic style of writing, and if it was a radical invention that is responsible for literacy as we know it, why is this so? Why are the other types of script, using symbols to represent either words or syllables, not just as effective as the alphabetic script?

We may assume that the more readers there are in proportion to the whole population, the more literate the population is. So the quantitative aspect of literacy depends upon how many persons out of a population can read and write. Sheer numbers are an important factor in full literacy. Those who can read by either a logographic or syllabic system, however, number comparatively few in any population. Only those who are especially trained, almost always persons whose full-time occupation is reading and writ-

grapheme
A letter or letter combination that represents the phoneme of a language, such as the graphemes c and s in the words "cite" and "sight" that represent the phoneme/s/ or the graphemes f and ph in "fish" and "photograph" that stand for the phoneme/f/.

ing, are able to enjoy the luxury of literacy. Such a situation we call "**craft literacy**."

craft literacy
Term applied to individuals like medieval scribes who copied over manuscripts in languages they did not understand, such as Irish scribes copying latin scripts.

What about the qualitative aspects of a script? What makes a particular type of writing efficient? "Efficiency" refers to how easily a person can read a particular script. What features of a script allow a large percentage of people of any ethnic, religious, or racial group to read it swiftly and effortlessly?

It must be granted that especially gifted persons can, by arduous training, make sense of virtually any script. If large numbers of people are to learn to read, however, they must learn to recognize the shapes of the written language and match them with the sounds they are designed to represent. Furthermore, if they are to read well, they must match signs with sounds almost instantaneously and virtually below the level of consciousness. With alphabetic reading, the written shapes are meaningless in themselves. The signs are not meant to represent objects or ideas. Those who read alphabetically, although they realize that the shapes have no inherent meaning, have learned a process that is not really a skill, or even a set of skills, but, rather, is a process that models language and thinking.

The primary act of reading, if it is to be enjoyed by large number of people, must be an easy, swift, and unconscious act. (Interpretation, finding the meaning of what one reads, is a different matter. We may say that interpreting meaning in writing is determining the difference between "what is written" and "what is meant.")

What then are the conditions necessary if a script is to fulfill the requirements for large numbers of persons to read easily and swiftly? First, ideally the symbols used to represent the sounds of a language should be *exhaustive;* that is, the written shapes should cover all the sounds of the language. The shapes must be sufficient in number to trigger the reader's memory of every distinctive sound—each phoneme—of the language. Amazingly, all the sounds of any language can be described and reduced to a fairly small number of phonemes, one phoneme

for one sound. If a system of writing were perfect, there would be no exceptions. No writing system is ideal, however, especially not that of English.

When we read the English word "knight," for instance, we have learned by listening to the way others say the word that it is pronounced "nite," not "kuh-nik-ta," as it was pronounced hundreds of years ago. The letters "-ght," represent a sound known as a "**velar fricative**." (The velar fricative is made with the back of the tongue on or near the soft palate. The sound is popularly known as a "guttural." Although the sound is prominent in German, it is no longer heard in English, except in Scottish dialects, as in the word "loch.")

The English writing system, as we're all aware, is less than perfect. But the script, which has only twenty-six symbols, is able in some fashion to account for all the sounds of the language. These twenty-six symbols—of letters—sometimes must represent more than one sound, though; for example, the "c" must stand for the "soft" sound at the beginning of "century" or "censure" as well as for the "hard" sound at the beginning of "cat" or "catalogue."

Second, for a script to be efficient, there should be no question as to what sound each shape represents; that is, the shapes should be *unambiguous*. In other words, each sign should trigger in the memory of the reader—which is what reading is all about—one sound, and one sound only. Again, if the system of writing were flawless, there would be no exceptions to the sound-symbol correspondences. There shouldn't be any times when the reader must guess at how to read a word or determine how to read it by how it is used in relation to other words. How do we know, for instance, the pronunciation of the word "bass"? Only when we see it with other words, in context. The word "bass" is read one way if it refers to a musical instrument, another way if it signifies a fish.

Third, the total *number of signs for the phonemes of the language must be small enough* that any reader can memorize all of them and relate them to all the

---

velar fricative

A sound made in the back of the tongue touching or near the soft palate as the "g" in "good" and the "k" in "king." The sound is not heard in modern English except in the Scottish "loch" meaning a lake."

sounds of the language. It is no wonder that only a few especially trained and gifted individuals can read a logographic script, in which symbols represent the words of the language. In English, even discounting many compound and scientific words, there are estimated to be some 600,000 words. Think of trying to memorize only a small number of the symbols for all the possible words in English!

It is not enough for us simply to remember the twenty-six shapes in the English alphabet. Once we learn our ABCs, we must associate these symbols with the sounds they stand for. Furthermore, in order to read fluently, we need to recognize these myriad sound-symbol connections, not in the neat, constant letters of the alphabet, an "abecedarium," but in the potentially limitless, irregular combinations of words and sentences. "The brain has been biologically encoded to contain a memory of these varieties as they occur acoustically in a spoken tongue. It has not been encoded to manage a corresponding variety of shapes" (Havelock, 1976, 23). When we think of reading from this perspective, we can only marvel at what an intellectual feat the process actually is.

So for reading to be within the reach of a great many people in a community, a script must necessarily be exhaustive, covering all distinctive sounds of the language; it must be unambiguous, ideally with each sound of the language being represented by one symbol only; and the number of signs standing for the sounds of the language must be small enough—generally between twenty and thirty—so that the human brain can memorize and process all the limitless combinations of signs that make up words and sentences.

Are these three conditions all that is necessary for literacy? Not quite. Full literacy, not craft literacy, is possible only when a fourth condition exists: an *early systematic reading instruction program,* and this program must be of a special kind. Instruction in reading must begin early enough that the child is able to internalize the process of connecting the sounds of a language with the symbols represent-ing them. This recognition of sound-symbol correspondences apparently must occur while the brain is plastic and has not fully concluded its growth, that is, before puberty. This habit of recog-nizing sound-symbol connections evidently must take place at the same time the brain is developing oral language, for which it is biologically pro-grammed. The codes of speaking and reading have to blend at a time when the child's brain is still in a formative stage. This is the optimum time for a child to learn how to read so that the act becomes an involuntary reflex.

The early systematic reading instruction pro-gram is thus the fourth condition for full literacy. "In short, a population is rendered literate when an edu-cational apparatus can be brought into being which is able to teach reading to very young children before they have been introduced to other skills. The adult who learns to read after his oral vocabulary is com-pleted rarely if ever becomes fluent" (Havelock, 1976, 24).

The Alphabet Versus the Syllabary

Why are the logographic and syllabic scripts not as well suited for widespread literacy as is the alphabetic script, according to the criteria estab-lished for an efficient script?

We can immediately see that the logographic scripts are unsuitable, because if we use a specific sym-bol for each word in a language we end up with far too many symbols to remember. We are either restricted to a very simple vocabulary, or if we do use a fairly large number of symbols for many words, only talented and highly talented people who continu-ally study and memorize the symbols will be able to read anything but the simplest messages.

There were many attempts to develop scripts before the Greeks devised a complete alphabetic script that represented both vowels and consonants. The Phoenicians invented a syllabic script, and so did the North Semitic tribes, from whose languages

Persian, Sanskrit, Aramaic, Hebrew, and Arabic have evolved. But the term "alphabet"—a word simply made up of the names for the first two letters of the Greek alphabet—should be applied only to the Greek system and to those scripts derived from it, the Roman and Cyrillic.

Why is the Greek system superior to the Phoenician syllabic system and the syllabaries descended from it? The answer lies in the script's ability to represent the two fundamental sounds of speech by written signs. Basically, scripts that use symbols for consonants only have no vowels and are thus "**unvocalized**."

unvocalized scripts

Scripts with consonants only, with no vowels, such as Hebrew.

If we represent the sounds of a language by syllables and these syllables by consonants only, we have scripts that are very difficult to make sense of. We, who have been brought up from childhood with the ideas of "vowels" and "consonants," may find it incomprehensible that these two concepts had to be invented. What was the result of the perception that speech was made up of two basic kinds of sounds and that these sounds could be represented in writing?

The Phoenician alphabet, we are told, also had letters representing sounds as did some syllabic systems, for instance, the Cypriot Greek syllabary (Thomas, 1992, 55). Much has been made of the fact that the Greeks added vowels to the Phoenician system, which consisted solely of consonants. Why did this happen? It seems as though the Phoenician language—like other Semitic languages—was a language that relied heavily on consonants while ancient Greek was made up of both consonant and vowel sounds.

> Certainly Phoenician in the written form, like other Semitic languages, did not have vowels, but then it did not need to do so for comprehension. Greek, on the other hand, did need vowel signs because (a) it has clusters of vowels in the middle of words (i.e. the stem), and (b) the inflected case-endings often consist of vowels or end with vowels, so that vowels may be absolutely essential to sense and grammatical construction. . . . In any case,

> when the Greeks adapted certain signs as vowel-letters, it is very likely that they *thought* they were hearing a vowel sound approximating to their vowels. (Thomas, 1992, 55)

As we "read" the syllables in a syllabary, we have to guess at missing vowels. Or, on the basis of prior teaching, we supply the vowels to create words. So we are right back where we started from, with ambiguous symbols. Such a situation does not make for fluent reading; rather, it becomes a difficult, often puzzling, and laborious task.

As the Greeks divided speech sounds into the two written elements of vowels and consonants and reduced each sound to its basic acoustic element—the phoneme—they invented an alphabetic script, a writing system obviously far more useful than the clumsy logographic and syllabic scripts. "In short, non-vocalized syllabaries require a little more effort, a little more time, on the part of the reader who deciphers accurately, than does the Greek system. To that extent, even at their best they are less efficient reading instruments" (Havelock, 1976, 32).

How the Alphabet Works

If we are to comprehend our writing system, we need to look closely at the alphabet and discover how it works.

The problem of an efficient script is that it must be at the same time both acoustic (we hear the sounds of language) and visual (we must be able to match letters with the sounds they stand for). To show the difference between an unvocalized script, in which there are no vowels, and an alphabetic script, which uses both consonants and vowels, we reproduce the first three words of the familiar nursery rhyme, "Jack and Jill went up the hill . . ." in both scripts (Havelock, 1976, 39–43).

First, we show an alphabetic script representation of the words to the nursery rhyme:

JAK AND JIL

Notice that in this phonemic version, we have omitted the unnecessary "c" from the word "Jack"

and the superfluous "l" from the double consonant in the word "Jill." (Remember, this is a phonemic rendering of the oral phrase; it is not the way we write it in a "conventional orthography.") For all of us who grew up with this nursery rhyme, and who have mastered the English alphabet and who have learned how to read, these symbols are instantly meaningful. Note that in this simple phrase, we have used nine symbols, of which only seven are different.

How might we write the same phrase, using an unvocalized system, one that uses no vowels?

$$J K N D J L$$

First of all, if we did not know that these symbols stand for the phrase "Jack and Jill," could we read it? This is a major shortcoming with an unvocalized script, for if we do not already know what the script says, we can make sense of it only with difficulty.

Now we can see quite clearly that this unvocalized phrase uses fewer signs than does the alphabetic phrase—only six symbols, of which five are unique. So it would appear that because this system uses fewer symbols, it is more efficient than the alphabetic phrase. But even though the unvocalized phrase is more economical than the alphabetic phrase by this measurement, the true test of a script's efficiency is how easily and unambiguously we can read it. The unvocalized script clearly fails this second criterion.

Results of the Invention of the Alphabet

So we have at our disposal the invention of an efficient script—a technology as radical and influential as the printing press or the computer chip. This discovery, like all major inventions, was not developed overnight. It took literally hundreds of years for its full potential to be realized. What has happened to the Greek alphabet since its invention?

How has it changed over the centuries? Is it still efficient? There is no doubt that the original Greek alphabet has been altered since its invention. But if the original Greek alphabet was superior, why did it

develop into the two other main phonemic alphabets, the **Roman (or Latin) alphabet** and the **Cyrillic alphabet** (used for Russian, Bulgarian, and certain other languages of the former Soviet Union)? Why, even with the modern Roman alphabet, do we have to add special marks to letters in words to show how to pronounce them?

In Spanish, for instance, we add a **diacritical mark**, the tilde (~) above the letter "n" to show how to pronounce a word like *señor* or *cañon*. In English, we solve the problem by adding the letter "y," for example, spelling the English word that comes from *canon* as "canyon." French places a diacritical mark, the cedilla, below the letter "c" to show that the sound is not the hard "k" sound but the soft, sibilant "s" sound, as in *garçon,* "boy."

We use other marks in addition to the letters themselves to indicate aspects of pronunciation, such as accent marks. In French, for example, we use the *accent ague* to show the stress of a syllable, as in the word cliché, for instance.

And why is it that the North Semitic unvocalized scripts have held their own in representing existing languages like Arabic? Why did Turkish replace the Greek alphabet after the fall of Constantinople to the Turks? Why is it that the script now used to write Hebrew, a language derived from the North Semitic, has replaced the Roman alphabet in modern Israel?

The answer lies in the fact that no script is ideal; none provides perfect correspondences between the signs of its written language and the possible sounds it is supposed to represent. This situation we call the law of "**residual ambiguity**." All scripts, even those of the major alphabetic systems, are to some degree ambiguous. There are several reasons for this.

First, the pronunciations of words may change over time, but written signs for the words may not have changed. Thus, spelling often lags behind pronunciation. The English word "bright," for instance, was one time pronounced as "brich-ta." We now say this word as "brite," but we still spell it the way it was first spelled phonetically hundreds of years ago.

Also, the alphabet was originally devised by the Greeks to reflect the distinctive sounds in their own language. Other languages, however, have sounds that do not exist in Greek. And likewise, languages other than English have sounds not found in English. German, for instance, has a sound in the word *Ich*—the velar fricative described above—that we do not have in English. In order to represent the sounds in their own languages, writers had to find new ways to symbolize the sounds by adding diacritical marks; or they simply assumed readers would be taught how to pronounce these words. Furthermore, as efficient as the Greek alphabet was, it did not account for all the sounds in Greek. Some residual ambiguities remained. Readers are required simply to learn from other native speakers how certain words are pronounced.

So the three major alphabetic systems—the Greek, Roman, and Cyrillic—all have exceptions, no matter what particular language they are used for, but the alphabet was never intended to be perfect.

> The function of the original model [the Greek alphabet] was not to replace a prior knowledge of spoken speech but to trigger a recall of that knowledge. Its effective use depended upon the requirement that the oral vocabulary of the reader first be fluent and educated. The alphabet was and is an instrument of acoustic recognition, and only that. It happens to be the most efficient so far devised by man. (Havelock, 1976, 55)

In effect, the alphabet activates the memory of the reader to associate written symbols with certain speech sounds. In order for the reader to use the alphabet for this purpose, though, the reader must first have a fully developed command of oral language.

Even though the Greek alphabetic script was effective, it did not represent all the dialects of Greek equally well. Why, among all Greek dialects at the time alphabet writing was developing, did the Athenian dialect become standard? The Greek language, as spoken and written by the literate citizens of Athens, became dominant because this *polis* (city-state) was the most important cultural and political force in Greece. Although in Athens both the eastern and western pronunciations had been in competition, it was the Attic—or Athenian—pronunciation that prevailed. Because of the sheer quantity as well as the high quality of Athenian writing, the alphabet that best represented the Athenian dialect "became the alphabet of all literate Greeks. The end result was that a choice technological in character imposed itself through influences political and cultural" (Havelock, 1976, 57, 58).

In short, the fact that the Greek alphabet was a marvelous invention was not the sole reason why the Athenian writing system became the standard. Rather, it was because the Attic alphabet was the writing system of the most influential city in Greece, in terms of both its type of government and its cultural achievements in architecture, literature, and philosophy.

Just as the Athenian writing system became the preeminent script in the east for cultural and political reasons so too did the Latin writing system became the dominant system for similar historical reasons. Greeks colonized sections of what is now Italy, bringing, as might be expected, the Greek writing system. Although some scholars believe that Latin speakers used an Etruscan version of the immigrant Greek system, this is not certain. It may be that the early speakers of Latin were pre–literate, just as the Greeks themselves had been before 750 B.C., and that they had an oral, poetic tradition. In any event, the early Romans readily adopted the Greek alphabetic system.

The Roman alphabet was later adapted to depict the sounds of Old English. But new symbols had to be added to indicate the sounds of Old English. The letter "c" came to stand for two sounds: the "hard c" and the "soft c," as in the modern words "call" and "censor." The letter "w"—or "double v"—was used by Norman scribes to provide a different sign for the sound represented by the letter "v." For the Old

English versions of the Roman alphabet, the runic letter þ ("thorn") was created to stand for both the unvoiced "th" sound in our modern word "theme," and the voiced "th," the sound in our word "them."

We discuss such matters not to show that the Greek alphabet and its adaptations are so full of exceptions that they must be hopelessly inadequate to the task of efficiently representing speech in writing. Rather, we point out these linguistic discrepancies to illustrate that no alphabet is perfect, that all languages exhibit residual ambiguity. No alphabet is able to depict all the sounds in a single language, much less to stand for language sounds not found in the original language. Furthermore, the choices made concerning alphabets are likely to be made not on the basis of rational linguistic considerations but, rather, as a result of political influences.

Why do letters not correspond perfectly on a one-to-one basis with the sounds of a language? Because languages change, and the fact that letters do not always reproduce the sounds of the language they represent is often a historical matter. We must accept "that etymologies [the histories of words] are part of the history of sound, not of letters, even if, when examined by the literate scholar today, the letters take on the appearance of being a function of the language. The conventions of the script . . . are theoretically one thing: the behavior of the spoken tongue is something else altogether" (Havelock, 1976, 62).

Readership in Ancient Times

In early Greece, stone and baked clay were the earliest surfaces for writing. The Greek historian Herodotus noted that parchment—that is, cured animal skin—was available for writing, but, as we can imagine, it was scarce and expensive. The Egyptians first used papyrus, the other basic writing surface, and from the available evidence, the Greeks used papyrus in Athens at least during the first half of the fifth century B.C. Waxed tablets were also used for making notes.

There is no doubt that without the printing press and a cheap writing surface, writing was difficult and limited. The idea that there were "books"—in our present-day idea of bound pages—available for general readership during ancient times is misinformed. The words *biblos* or *biblyos* refer not to our modern, many-page books but to papyrus. In order to create a surface for writing extended texts, people would connect several sheets of papyrus by gumming them together at the edges. This made a continuous surface for written material that could conveniently be rolled up for carrying or stuffing into a pigeonhole. Unfortunately, finding one's place after leaving off reading required unrolling the scroll of papyrus sheets until it appeared. Not exactly a "pocket book" that could be slipped into one's toga. (Ironically, in order to find our place in a manuscript on a computer, we must again "scroll" up or back to find the section we want.)

As we can see, early reading was neither a simple nor an easy pastime. Rapid reading by a great number of people was simply not the case. Although the alphabet existed, the shortage of writing materials and the lack of standardization in writing and spelling, which was made possible by the printing press, led to a very limited readership indeed. It would be centuries before the potential of the alphabetic system for extensive literacy was to be fully realized:

> Alphabetic literacy, in order to overcome the limitation of method and so achieve its full potential, had to await the invention of the printing press. The original achievement, the Greek one, had solved an empirical problem by applying abstract analysis. But the material means for maximizing the result required the assistance of further inventions and had to await a long time for it. . . . The energy of the alphabet . . . had to await the assistance provided by the dawning scientific advance in Europe in order to be fully released. (Havelock, 1976, 73)

The Consequences of Literacy

How far is literacy an agent of change? Today, literacy is equated with high culture and literacy rates are assumed to correlate with cultural activity: in other words, literacy is consciously or unconsciously equated with civilization. It is not always clear whether the

number of 'illiterates' is lamented because literacy helps people fill in forms, or get jobs, or read books and enlarge their cultural experience. But at any rate, the range of possibilities underlines how much literacy has come to be identified with modern civilization and modern values. Literacy now bears a heavy burden of expectation. The UNESCO literacy campaigns aim to eliminate illiteracy totally, in the hope that literacy will promote economic development, rational thought and scientific endeavour in the Third World. No one would deny that the written word is of fundamental importance to the modern world, and that someone without literacy faces extreme difficulties. The problem is whether—or how far—literacy can be the main agent of change in the transformation. Or does it rather reflect ands strengthen tendencies already there? (The failure of literacy campaigns in the Third World and elsewhere suggest that literacy is very much more complex.)

(Thomas, 1992, 16.)

What were the long-range consequences of the invention of the alphabet and of the spread of literacy throughout the Western world? In what ways was full literacy—the ability of large numbers of people, not just an elite few, to read—destined, after many centuries, to permeate and influence every aspect of society: culture, religion, law, politics, science, and even government?

If we are to understand this transformation, though—a change in the very character of the Western mind—we need to review the background of this momentous transformation from an oral to literate culture.

We attribute the invention of the alphabet and the potential for full literacy to the ancient Greeks, but one man, the Greek philosopher Plato, as spokesman for a new kind of written, prosaic language—in direct opposition to the preeminent oral poetic language of the day, found primarily in the epics of Homer, the *Iliad* and *Odyssey*—almost single-handedly introduced a radically new way of using language. Particularly in *The Republic,* Plato makes a persuasive case for a rational, logical, abstract, and what we would call today "scientific" discourse, one with novel elements of prose such as analysis, classification, definition, cataloguing, and arguing from cause and effect.

Homer's Poetry

Who was Homer? And from our reading of his epics what was Homer? What do his narrative poems have to do with the traditions of orality and literacy?

First, who was Homer? Little is known about his life since there were few writers around who could record his biography. We do have a few references to him by writers in antiquity. Hellanicus, an early Ionian Greek writer, placed him in the twelfth century B.C. and wrote that from Homer's vivid description of the battles in the *Iliad* he must have been a witness to the Trojan War. Herodotus (c. 490–420 B.C.), the "father of history," placed him during the ninth century B.C. and, according to Herodotus, "four hundred years before my time and not more" (Kitto, 1991, 44). That's about all there is to the answer to the question of who Homer was as a person.

More importantly we need to ask the question what was Homer? And what influences did his epics have upon early Greek life? The *Iliad* and the *Odyssey*, we are told, formed the bible of the Greeks for centuries and were the basis of education, both for formal schooling and informal instruction for all citizens. Professional lecturers traveled from city to city, accepting contributions, and performing selected passages from Homer's work. It appears that Homer's poems affected Greeks from all walks of life—artists, other poets, philosophers, and common people as well. Even the great dramatist Aeschylus remarked that his plays were merely "slices from Homer's banquet" (Kitto, 1991, 45). In effect, Homer's epics united all the citizens of the *poleis* (city-states)—in spite of their constant disagreements and skirmishes—into a single, proud people.

Now to fundamental questions about the epics themselves. Was Homer an illiterate poet? Were the epics purely oral songs recorded when they could finally be written down? Did Homer—living during the arrival of alphabetic writing—use writing to construct the epics from songs performed over generations and possibly centuries? What do the answers

to these questions reveal about the oral and written cultures and the relationships of one to the other?

If the very long and complicated epics were memorized and then performed by illiterate bards, how could the singers possibly have remembered them? The *Iliad,* for instance, consists of some 17, 000 lines of regular poetry, with each line consisting of six beats of feet, each foot generally with one accented and two unaccented stresses, known as dactylic hexameter.

But what if the bards hadn't *memorized* the poems but rather *improvised* them as they went along? For the scholar Milman Parry, this was precisely what they must have done. He based his finding on his study of the constantly recurring "ornamental epithets" in the epics, such as Hera, "the white-armed goddess"; Agamemnon, "lord of men" and "wide-ruling"; Achilles, "lord of men" and "wide ruling"; and dawn, "rosy-fingered." Surely the epithets are colorful, but they served a much more practical purpose. To keep the lines of poetry regular, the bards improvised by choosing the appropriate epithet to finish a line of poetry. "In other words, the particular epithet chosen by the poet may have nothing to do with, for example, whether Achilles is "brilliant" or "swift-footed" at this particular point in the poem—the choice depends on which epithet fits the meter" (Knox, 1991, 15). The epithets, then, "offer the improvising bard different ways of fitting the name of the god, hero, or object into whatever section of the line is left after he has, so to speak, filled up the first half—that too, quite possibly, with another formulaic phrase" (Knox, 1991, 15).

So we may have an answer to the question of whether the bards recited from memory or improvised the poems as they performed them. But a final question nags us. It can't be denied that the epics were at one time written down. We have them in our hands today. Did Homer merely dictate his oral poems, or did he use the newly developed skill of writing in constructing them? For Parry's collaborator and

successor, Albert B. Lord, the answer is an unequiv-
ocal "no." An illiterate bard could not at the same
time be able to compose in writing. Claims Lord: "It
is conceivable that a man might be an oral poet in
his younger years and a written poet later in life, but
it is not possible that he be *both* an oral and written
poet at one given time in his career. The two by their
nature are mutually exclusive" (2000, 129). The two
could not possibly combine to form a third "transi-
tional" language technique.

In response to Lord's contention, scholars
responded that no scribe in the eighth century B.C.
could take dictation fast enough, and since writing
was in its infancy, the act of writing was physically
difficult. Furthermore, how could a poet remember
such a complex and lengthy text of intricate poetry
without the aid of writing?

What are we to make of this "Homeric question"? The contemporary consensus is that the great
poems were composed by a single bard, building
upon an oral tradition many years old. Anyone who
has read the *Iliad* or *Odyssey* can give witness to the
directness, energy, and excitement of the epics. They
are simply great reads! As with other great folk epics,
like the Old English *Beowulf*, for instance, they were
songs, presented before audiences who would accept
nothing less than rousing poetic stories. It seems
evident that a single poet—call him Homer—may at
one time have used the new invention of writing to
construct over a period of years the final edifices of
the epics.

A recent translator of the *Iliad*, Robert Fagles,
describes the end result of what we read today, a text
in writing of an oral poem, shaped by illiterate bards
into a precious, written book.

> Here the performer . . . may have known a rudimen-
> tary form of writing. And writing may have lent to
> his work some qualities we associate with texts in
> general—idiosyncracies at times, and pungency
> and wit—and with the *Iliad* in particular, its archi-
> tectonics, its magnificent scale, and the figure of
> Achilles . . . So the original form of Homer's work,

while a far cry from a work of literature as we know it now, is not exactly a song either, pure and simple. It may be more the record of a song, or what Marianne Moore would call a "simulacrum of spontaneity" (Fagles, 1991, ix, x).

What was gained by writing down the oral epic? The spoken words were themselves preserved. And possibly the technique of writing helped to construct the text. But what was lost? The immediate, face-to-face, improvised oral performance of a great testament to a whole culture. The result is of literacy meeting and responding to orality, sharing both traditions but producing something completely original.

In what ways was an expository, rational language different from the oral, poetic narrative of Homeric epics? And how was it that writing was chiefly responsible for the invention of this novel, prosaic mindset? In order for Plato to set in place this new style of language, he needed to supplant the traditional language, that of the orally transmitted, poetic epics of Homer, the *Iliad* and *Odyssey*.

What were the characteristics of the Homeric epics—both of content and of language—that Plato's language replaced? First of all and fundamentally, the Homeric epics were poetic, and they were transmitted orally through performances by professional bards. Furthermore, although the public presentations were entertaining, their primary purpose was to teach; that is, they were "didactic." We need to emphasize these elements because in present-day society, poetry does not have such a crucial role. Many people dismiss poetry as a "frill." Even though some audiences may enjoy public poetry readings, the number of people in attendance is far fewer than the number at presentations of the epics or at the productions of Greek plays, such as *Antigone, Oedipus Rex,* and *Medea.* Though modern poetry may reveal "lessons" to its readers and audiences, few poets would hold that the contemporary purpose of poetry is to educate. And certainly, the poems we do enjoy today seldom are long, narrative epics. The poetic epics of

Homer's era had a much different place in society than does poetry today.

Because the Homeric epics were handed down orally, the bards who improvised them in performances and the people in the audience who learned them by heart needed a type of language they could easily recall. The ancient Greeks were totally non-literate, or since they lived in an era before print, we might say they were preliterate. They had no texts of the epics—except in their minds—with which to refresh their memories.

Furthermore, the epics were instructive: They were created to pass on to citizens a certain world-view, a common history they needed to share in order to survive as a cohesive people. But how was such a tradition passed on among people who could neither read nor write? A common core of beliefs can be handed down only through language in some kind of permanent and unalterable form. In a literate culture, such as ours, customs and usages are transmitted to a great extent through formal education, through books, written laws and decrees, and through libraries. But among preliterate people, like the ancient Greeks, since there was no writing system available during the time of Homer, this practice of conveying written records was not possible.

The only recourse for the culture's preservation is through the living memories of human beings. But learning the whole body of a long epic is an amazing feat. In Homer's time, the bard, the person who had learned the epic and presented it over several performances, had to take advantage of the techniques of memorization, of the available mnemonic devices. We know it is easier to commit to memory a regular, rhyming poem than it is to memorize a long passage of abstract prose, just as it is with a long, poetic narrative.

What characteristics of long poems allowed the bards to remember and improvise them? First of all, the bards memorized certain set pieces, such as battle scenes, long speeches, and descriptions of objects like the famous rendering of the Shield of

Achilles. At the same time, as we have discussed, they memorized many ornamental epithets, which were inserted in lines of poetry to make the meter fit. The epic, then, is made up of continually recurring rhythms, images, and words. To reinforce the effects of the verse, musicians frequently accompanied the poems with simple, repetitive rhythms produced on a popular musical instrument, the lyre. All these rhythmic elements—verbal and musical—contributed to make the poetic presentation pleasurable and, at the same time, more easily understood and remembered than would be prose passages. The whole production, we are told, was aimed at drawing the spectators into a highly emotional, psychologically satisfying experience. We might liken this participation to that at a highly emotional production of a TV program, movie, rock concert, or play. The rhythms and repetitive body movements of the bard had an emotional influence upon the members of the audience, providing a release from tension and anxiety. As a result, the performance often created something like a hypnotic effect, casting a spell upon the members of the audience and creating an intimate linkage between the didactic purpose of the narrative and a complementary sensual experience.

Since the epics needed to be learned and understood not by just a few gifted members of the audience but also by ordinary people, the body of the epics consisted not of abstract rules and prosaic statements—which are nearly impossible to memorize—but of a series of connected tales. We are all aware of how much easier it is to remember stories with characters in dramatic events than it is to keep in mind expository statements. The epics consist of many connected episodes, all related in an overarching grand story. The characters do not think about their motives and behavior, as characters in modern prose fiction do; rather they perform one action after another, without apparent conscious thought. And the primary characters—for example, the great warrior Achilles—are not just ordinary citizens. Since the primary aim of the epic was to educate, to teach

laws and customs of the culture, then the chief characters need to be outstanding persons in high offices whose actions are directly related to two basic kinds of laws of supreme importance to Greek culture: public law, the *nomos,* and family or private "law," the *ethos,* the Greek term from which we derive the modern word "ethics." In other words, the characters are "political" in the most fundamental sense of the word. These exemplary men and women, such as the Trojan hero Hector, perform passionate acts that are deeply felt by all members of the society. These political leaders have major roles in the epics "so the things they do will send out vibrations into the farthest confines of society, and the whole apparatus becomes alive and performs motions which are paradigmatic" (Havelock, 1963, 168).

A great deal has been made of the fact that characters in the ancient Greek epics and plays are "highborn" and "noble." When Arthur Miller's play *Death of a Salesman* was first produced, critics noted that because the chief character, Willy Loman, is not a "noble" hero but rather a "common man," the play technically—in the original Greek sense—could not be a tragedy. But the characters in the ancient Greek works were not chosen for snobbish reasons; they were chosen because their actions teach valuable lessons on how *not* to behave as well as on *how* to behave. "In sum, the saga [any long narrative] in order to do its job for the community and offer an effective paradigm of social law and custom, must deal with those acts which are conspicuous and political. And the actors who alone can furnish these paradigms in this kind of society we designate as 'heroes.' The reason for the heroic paradigm is in the last resort not romantic but functional and technical" (Havelock, 1963, 168). We might make the concept of the tragic hero more meaningful by reflecting on the lives and deaths of prominent political "heroes" such as Mahatma Gandhi, John F. Kennedy, and Martin Luther King, Jr.

The heroes in the Greek oral epics and plays thus represented the mores of all citizens. For these

preliterate people, the heroes epitomized the most respected men in society. The members of the audience observed the noble characters participating in an almost endless series of formal ceremonies surrounding births, marriages, great battles, deaths, and funerals. They saw how highborn characters behave during these key rituals, and they themselves learned how to act in such conventional public and private events.

What is the purpose for this endless chronicle of short, episodic milestones in a heroic character's life? This narrative strategy is again necessary for ease of memorization. A single great story can only be remembered if it is made up of a number of related episodes. Therefore, the events in the epic are all complete and satisfying in themselves. Action succeeds action in a seemingly unbroken chain, without any authorial generalizations (such as "Achilles was a great warrior"). In the epic, incident after incident deals with specific warriors—a great many are named—fighting in numerous battles. These events are presented without coordinate or subjunctive conjunctions (such grammatical forms were not used in the epics) in what is called a "paratactic" sentence pattern: The basic pattern in this oral story is shown by words and phrases like "next" and "then."

Furthermore, the oral epic is made up of a great number of visual images, in contrast with the present-day practice in nonpoetic writing of using abstractions and generalizations. The reason for creating these elements in the epic—for stringing all the episodes together without general statements and making overwhelming use of concrete details and visual images—is to enable the audience to remember the stories and, through an emotional, rhythmic, spellbinding performance, learn the political and family laws of the people. "Hence neither technical information [such as directions for navigating boats] nor moral judgment [such as pointing out that Achilles refuses to fight because his pride has been wounded] can be presented reflectively in the saga as true generalization couched in the language of uni-

versals" (Havelock, 1963, 181). Without the aid of written records, the ancient Greeks, although they could remember the exciting doings of great heroes, were not expected to memorize long, complex prose statements. Besides, we have no evidence of such writing in Greek oral literature.

In short, the oral epic performance was likened to a dreamlike state: the audience came under the spell of the poetic narrative as performed by the bard with his physical gestures and with musical accompaniment on a lyre. This spell contrasts vividly with prosaic language, which is reflective, rational, and unemotional and which can be created only when people are literate, when they can write down information and think about it, when they no longer need mnemonic devices for memorization. Poetic language obviously has its drawbacks, but before we are too quick to dismiss it as a frill in society, we should acknowledge that it was preeminent in one area, which it did superbly well: it taught citizens public and private laws while at the same time supplying a complete emotional life. "It was a life without self-examination, but as a manipulation of the resources of the unconscious in harmony with the conscious it was unsurpassed" (Havelock, 1963, 190).

The Birth of Prose in Western Language and Thought

Now we turn to a consideration of how the invention of the Greek alphabet and full literacy, not the craft literacy of a few, created a revolution in language, literally changing the content, vocabulary, and syntax of the Greek language and indeed the mindset of Western culture. The introduction of Greek letters was to alter forever the qualities of Western culture, creating a gulf between all alphabetic cultures and those of peoples who were not literate or who had a nonalphabetic script.

Is this an extreme statement? Perhaps, but how long did it take for this revolution in language to occur? Was a single person responsible? And in what

specific ways did this new language take the place of oral poetry in the Homeric epic, a kind of language so deeply embedded in the Greek culture that it had held sway for hundreds of years? That Greek literary language eventually changed from a concrete, visual language to a rational, abstract, "scientific" language is not an outlandish declaration. The transformation did not happen overnight; it took more than three hundred years, from about 700 to 400 B.C., for the "new" Greek language to be fully developed.

No one person could be solely responsible for this change, but we generally acknowledge that the Greek philosopher Plato describes in considerable detail the elements of this new language in *The Republic,* thus making his thoughts available to a wide range of sophisticated readers. Before Plato, a number of Greek philosophers had attempted to work out, step-by-step, these ideas about a kind of abstract language. These pioneering thinkers were the pre-Socratic philosophers and Socrates himself, the mentor of Plato. In *The Republic,* Plato spoke of this age-old debate between poetic language and the abstract language employed by philosophers: "Our defense, then when we are reminded that we banished poetry from our state, must be that its character was such as to give us good grounds for so doing and that the argument required it. But in case we are condemned for being insensitive and bad mannered, let us add that there is an old quarrel between philosophy and poetry" (Plato, 2003, 351). Although we usually credit Plato with most effectively articulating a new prose discourse, he was not the only advocate for rational, abstract thought; he was, however, undoubtedly the most significant. Plato was "one of those thinkers in whom seminal forces of a whole epoch sprang to life. Plato thinks the unconscious thoughts of his contemporaries. He gives to the intellectual currents of his age their direction and drive. He sought to create the current of intellectualism itself" (Havelock, 1963, 277).

We are compelled to ask the same questions about Plato as we did of Homer, with answers to put

human faces on these legendary figures and to achieve a degree of satisfaction in understanding how each represented a distinctly different kind of knowing and fundamentally different kind of language.

Who was Plato? And from that which we know about his life and times and from what he wrote, what was Plato? We need ask another question of him, though, one that has nagged us for centuries. Why did Plato distrust poetry so strenuously that he banished the poet from his Utopian Republic?

Who then was Plato? And how did his life and times affect what he believed? We know so much more about Plato than the shadowy Homer obviously because Plato lived in a time of advanced literacy. We need to remember that Plato—flourishing in the fifth and fourth centuries B.C.—lived in a very different world than did Homer, who we are told existed during the eighth century B.C., some 400 years before Plato. Homer lived during a time of oral tradition, on the cusp between orality and high literacy. The Greeks of Plato's time, we surmise, "were deeply attached to their past, but it was a distant timeless past, the age of gods and heroes, which attracted them and which they were never tired of learning about from Homer and the tragic poets" (Finley, 1972, 13).

Plato, of the bluest blood, came from a distinguished family with many political connections. Through his stepfather, he had a link to Pericles, the statesman who gave his name to the great age of Athenian history.

One of the most important long-lingering events of Plato's life was the Peloponnesian War between Sparta and Athens, which began in the spring of 431 B.C., just before he was born and lasted until he was twenty-three. Plato, as a child and young man, grew up in a city almost constantly at war. But it was no usual small-scale, one-day, mini-war between small city-states. To give us some idea of the continued ferocity of the conflict, we quote a description from a modern scholar:

> What Kagan [Donald Kagan, author of *The Peloponnesian War*, 2004] rightly calls "a funda-

mental departure" from this tradition [of small, day-long almost predictable skirmishes], not only in scope, duration, and complexity but also in savagery and bitterness . . . the result, Kagan emphasizes, was a cycle of cruelty and reprisal that ended in a "collapse in the habits, institutions, beliefs, and restraints that are the foundations of civilized life. . . . In the end, the great standard-bearer of Greek civilization itself, Athens collapsed. Bankrupt and imploding with civil strife after nearly three decades of fighting, it was finally defeated by an alliance of Sparta and Persia, the traditional enemies of the Greeks. (Mendelsohn, 2004, 79, 80)

We can only imagine the effects of such a vicious war upon the young, impressionable Plato, who only dimly understood what was happening.

The war ended in 404 B.C. in defeat and humiliation for Athens, followed by an oligarchic revolution. A commission of thirty, known as The Thirty, was set up to frame a new constitution, but instead, the members used their power as tyrants to settle old scores. The Thirty were eventually driven out and the democratic constitution restored.

But the city fathers did one thing Plato could never forget nor forgive. They put to death his friend and mentor Socrates on the charges of impiety and corrupting the youth of the city. How did these unstable times and the death—on trumped-up charges—of his mentor affect Plato? We have Plato's own words from his *Seventh Letter,* written when he was an old man about the years when he was in his mid-twenties.

At first, wrote Plato, he had expected to go into politics, to reform society and rule justly. After The Thirty fell and the constitution was changed, again he felt, less keenly though, a desire to enter government. But these were "troublesome times," he wrote, and he was "not surprised that vengeance should sometimes be excessive in a revolution." The crowning evil, however, was the execution of Socrates. He wrote, "Unfortunately, however, some of those in power brought my friend Socrates to trial on a monstrous charge, the last that could be made against him, the charge of impiety; and he was condemned and executed" (Lee, 2003, x, xi).

For Plato, the death of Socrates (recounted in Plato's dialogue, "The Apology") meant a final disillusionment with contemporary politics. The more he studied politicians and laws and customs of the day, and the older he got, the more nearly impossible it seemed to him for one to govern rightly. As a result of these circumstances, Plato made a decision to give up his long-held desire to enter politics and to devote his life to the study of philosophy. In old age, Plato wrote:

> I was forced, in fact, to the belief that the only hope of finding justice for society or for an individual lay in true philosophy, and that mankind will have no respite from trouble until either real philosophers gain political power or politicians become by some miracle true philosophers. (Lee, 2003, xviii)

During the years after Socrates' death, Plato was said to have traveled to Egypt and Phoenicia, but he spent a good deal of time in Athens since we are told he served in the Athenian army for three campaigns. In 388 to 387 he visited South Italy, possibly to meet some Pythagorean philosophers, who influenced him strongly, as we can see from his opinions about the value of the study of mathematics.

In 386 he returned to Athens, founding the Academy—a model for future universities in the West—where he taught for the rest of his life. The Academy as we might suspect was founded as a school for statesmen, where a "new type of politician might learn to be a philosopher ruler" (Lee, 2003, xix). He died in 347 B.C.

From his life experiences and writings, we have some understanding of Plato's views toward the education of the ideal philosopher-ruler, pointedly in his dissertation on the education of politicians, the *Republic*. In this book, we also find his position about the place of the poet and poetry in his educational scheme in Part X: "Theory of Art."

For Plato, poetry "has no serious value and claim to truth," and anyone who hears poetry must fear its effects. Art and poetry appeal to and represent the lower, less rational part of our nature. We should not admit the poet to a properly run state "because he wakens and encourages and strengthens the lower elements in the mind to the detriment of reason, which is like giving power and political control to the worst elements in a state and ruining the better element." Argues Plato, "the gravest charge against poetry remains. It has a terrible power to corrupt even the best character, with very few exceptions" (Plato, 2003, 348, 349).

For Plato, poetic language is an imitation of what is real, twice removed, as is the poet's treatment of a bed, copied from the carpenter's bed, which in turn is a copy of the ideal, abstract form of bed-ness. Furthermore, since the philosopher-king must rule by reason, through dialectic dialogue and logic, the passions of pleasure and pain engendered by the poet have no place in Plato's realm of rationality and reason.

In effect, the new rational, abstract thinking mode of perceiving reality—a language Plato was developing as he went along—was totally at odds with Homer's emotional, rhythmic, rhyming, concrete, figurative, and ambiguous mode of feeling. These two ways of knowing, thought by many to be irreducibly different and representing two dissimilar kinds of language, we know today as expository and literary. Some maintain that Plato's way of thinking and using language carried the day and is still ascendant in contemporary Western culture.

One of the most strikingly innovative discoveries contributing to Plato's new way of thinking appears in the Greek concept of "psyche," the entity that we might define as "soul" and sometimes call "personality." By the end of the fifth century B.C., some Greek philosophers began to talk about their "souls," which they saw as autonomous and which had distinctive selves and personalities. The Greek word *psyche* may also be translated as "ghost," not the scary Halloween ghost of our culture but rather a "spirit who thinks." In this view, an individual psyche is not only separate from all other psyches, but it is also capable of "thinking" as well as acting. In the Homeric epics, the characters did not think; they acted forthrightly and did not think about their actions. Such thinking could be accomplished only through abstractions. But there was no abstract thinking in the epics, certainly no thinking about thinking because this mental act and the words to describe it had not yet been devised. What we now call "metacognition," that is "thinking about thinking" or "metalinguistics," that is "thinking about language," was simply not present in the ancient Greek mind and therefore couldn't be expressed in the Greek language. So this psyche not only thinks, it must think about something, and this something was the result of rational thought. Finally, this thinking psyche was infinitely precious, an essence absolutely unique in the whole realm of nature.

Thus, Plato's opposition to the poetic experience involved two assumptions: there is a psyche (personality) that thinks, and there is a body of knowledge that is not *felt* but rather *thought about* and knowable. How did this philosophic discovery of the individual self, the psyche, contribute to a new kind of language? This individual psyche has the power to think, to cogitate, and to know. These mental powers are diametrically opposed to the poetic ability to see, to hear, and to feel. We see this separation in its clearest form in the dialectic method of questioning by Socrates, who asks questions to compel speakers to think about what they have said. But the questions are of a special kind. When Socrates queries his listener, he urges him to repeat what he has said and then to explain what he meant by his words. By this process, Socrates arouses the speaker from an unsubstantiated emotional opinion, which is likened to the "dream state" of poetry. Socrates, by his use of the dialectic, in which he insists that the speaker think about what he has said, forces the speaker to think abstractly. For instance, instead of identifying emo-

tionally with the great hero Achilles, Socrates' student is now asked to think about Achilles' behavior and make a general statement summarizing the warrior's actions. Did he act childishly? Bravely? With justification?

As the speaker in the Socratic dialogue repeats what he has said and then thinks about his original statement, explaining what he meant, he is interpreting. The idea of "interpretation" is also new to Western thought. Socrates says to the speaker, "Tell me what you just said. Say it again." He is requiring the speaker to restate his original position. And this time, the speaker needs to say it in prosaic, rational, and abstract language. Aha! The clever teacher educates his pupil how to think by using a newly devised thought process.

Thus is born "**hermeneutics**," the science and methodology of interpretation. And with it, the ability to think about language, literally to think "beyond language," which we now consider an extremely high level mental ability. In order to think this way with and about language, though, we need a fresh vocabulary. If we are to make a declaration, to say that "Something is _____," we need the verb "is." For example, if we wish to make a general statement about Achilles, such as "Achilles is a great hero," then we are obliged to use the verb "is." In the ancient Greek language and in the Homeric epics, the verb "is" does not exist. Why is this fact significant? In the *Iliad,* we know how heroes like Achilles and Hector behave by observing their actions through numerous episodes. Because the language used to recount the events refers to concrete things, we can think only concretely, not abstractly. But if we want to make a general statement—which the language of the epic does not allow us to do—we need to use the verb "is": "The hero is brave." "He is compassionate." And "He is law abiding." With the invention of alphabetic writing, we are now able to draw from many examples and make a general statement. We have learned how to generalize. Instead of describing concrete objects and creatures poetically, we are

hermeneutics
The science and methodology of interpretation, especially of Scripture.

now able to construct abstract statements about what we see and hear. With this radical idea of being able to see ourselves "outside" language and thus to think about language—rather than being passively moved by an emotionally overpowering, poetic performance—we can now think about a thing per se, the thing "in itself." The phrase "per se," which literally means "by itself," is another element of this new prosaic language that allows us to think abstractly. Instead of showing characters in a number of episodes acting heroically, we can now say "Heroism 'per se' is a quality to be desired in a warrior."

At the heart of this linguistic revolution, however, is Plato's theory of forms. "Here is a new form of discourse and a new kind of vocabulary offered to the European mind" (Havelock, 1963, 260). Plato's theory of the forms may best be explained by his own example in *The Republic* of the different levels of abstraction for the word "bed."

1. *The original, the form Bed.* At the first and highest level of abstraction, in the realm of pure essence, is the unique and eternal form Bed, corresponding to our word "bed." This form, however, is not what we call a generalization or concept, which we as humans are able to create. As human beings, we do not create forms. They already exist. We can only apprehend them through our intellect. "So the Forms are not the creation of the intellect, and this means that the 'objects' represented by such linguistic devices as 'the itself per se' are not the creations of the intellect either" (Havelock, 1963, 263). Today, we commonly translate Plato's forms as "ideas," the notion that forms the basis of the branch of philosophy known as Idealism.

2. *Secondhand copy of Bed by a craftsman.* The worker who makes a physical bed may create any number of kinds of beds—four-posters, sleigh beds, rope beds, ad infinitum—but all are derived from the abstract form ("idea") Bed.

3. *Thirdhand copy of a copy of Bed by a poet or artist.*
The artist, be it a poet, painter, or sculptor,
copies the copy of the form Bed made by the
craftsman. Thus, the poet deals with the essential form Bed at thirdhand, as a copy of a copy
of the original form.

What is the result of this revolutionary concept
of forms, the abstract essences of all creatures, things,
and ideas? With the discovery of the abstract forms,
we can now think about such matters, and we are
thus compelled to create new words to describe
these forms. We can think and write abut such
abstractions as "beautiful," "just," and "good" and
about their opposites, "ugly," "unjust," and "evil."
We can also think about ideas such as "double,"
"half," "great," "small," "light," and "heavy." We can
think about numerical notions such as "odd," "even,"
"square," three types of "angles," and "diameter." In
other words, we can think about and describe the natural world by equations, laws, formulas, and categories. These ideas are timeless. They are completely
different from the actions of characters in epics,
which occur during periods of time and are thus "time
conditioned." For the first time, the theory of forms
"announced the arrival of a completely new level of
discourse which as it became perfected was to create in turn a new kind of experience in the world—
the reflective, the scientific, the technical, the
theological, the analytic" (Havelock, 1963, 267).

What do we call this person who is able to think
abstractly? The word for a person able to employ fully
this new discourse, so antithetical to the poetic dic-
tion of the Homeric epics, is "philosopher." The
word "philosopher" first appears in works from early
in the fourth century B.C., but the verb "philosophize"
is found in works from the last quarter of the fifth
century B.C.; the best-known use of the word is by
Pericles in his famous *Funeral Oration:* "Our love of
what is beautiful does not lead to extravagance; our
love of the things of the mind [to philosophize]
does not make us soft [effeminate]" (Thucydides,
1972, 147). It was, however, Plato who first used the

word "philosopher" in *The Republic* to describe the kind of person who epitomized the idea of a rational thinker "simply as a man who is prepared to challenge the concrete over the consciousness, and to substitute the abstract" (Havelock, 1963, 281).

The modern etymology given for the word "philosopher," as literally meaning in English "one who loves wisdom," is not only insufficient but actually misleading. Havelock translates *phil-* not as "love" but as a "psychic urge, drive, thirst, all consuming desire," and *sophia* not as "wisdom" but rather as "capacity for abstract thinking." A more accurate literal rendition for "philosopher," then would be "one who has an unconquerable urge to deal with abstractions," that is, a person we now label—minus all the negative connotations—an intellectual" (Havelock, 1963, 282).

Fundamental Consequences of the Alphabet

After this examination of how Plato, because of the prior invention of the alphabet and of a written language, could reveal the vital existence of this new rational, abstract language, what can we say about the influence of the alphabet and literacy upon the cognition and psychology of the Western mind?

On the one hand, the invention of the alphabet may have actually transformed the makeup of mental processes in Western civilization. "What the new script may have done in the long run was to change somewhat the content of the human mind" (Havelock, 1976, 46). The psychological effect of the Greek alphabet was that the twenty-odd symbols, once learned, were pushed down below the level of awareness and virtually forgotten. Once internalized, the symbols allowed persons to read easily and quickly. With the Greek alphabet, the burden of remembering thousands of symbols—one for each word—was lifted. Now the energy once expended on memorizing symbols was made available for thinking about new thoughts and writing them down so they could be consulted again and again without wor-

rying about remembering them. In the process, we gained the opportunity not just to memorize the same old stories, familiar myths, plays, and long narrative poems, without the aid of written records, but to contribute to the expansion of knowledge available to the human mind.

Although some scholars argue that the alphabet literally changed the cognitive and psychological processes of the Western mind, others believe that rather than actually altering minds, the alphabet and literacy provided novel "models" for thinking about language and ways of using language in writing as well as in speaking. In other words, through reading, we learn strikingly new ways of thinking, speaking, and writing, including thinking "about" language. "The magic of writing," states David Olson,

> arises not so much from the fact that writing serves as a new mnemonic device, an aid to memory, as from the fact that writing may serve an important epistemological function. Writing not only helps us remember what we thought and said but also invites us to see what was thought and said in a new way. It is a cliché to say that there is more to writing than the abc's and more to literacy than the the ability to decode words and sentences. (1994, xv)

In sum, writing has either altered the human mind or, with the same result, opened the mind to new ways of thinking, speaking, and writing. Writing became a "technology of the intellect" (Goody, 1986). Through writing, for instance, we can make lists of words and then group the words into certain categories, thus utilizing the language skills of classification and generalization. In ancient oral poetry, for instance, we find lists not as separate kinds of language but as language embedded within the poetic narrative, such as the list of warriors from different parts of Greece in the *Iliad*. The primitive classification, rather than being an integral part of the epic, may have served as a forerunner of one part of the whole logical, specialized, and cumulative tradition of Athenian prose of the sixth century B.C.

If we consider the notion that reading and writing serve as models for thinking, we notice that writing is not simply speech written down word for word. All we have to do to recognize this fact is to tape-record friends chatting. When we play the conversation back, we should not be amazed at how unlike purposeful writing casual speech is—lacking cohesion and full of repetitions and false starts. Rather than merely transcribing speech, then, writing serves as a tentative structure of language, showing us the infinite variety of sentences and words available. "Learning to read and write is, therefore," argues Olson, "learning to hear and think about one's language in a new way. Consequently, it may alter speech practices as well as report them. This is what makes learning to read both important and difficult" (1999, 132).

In short, writing and reading may very well provide models for more prosaic uses of language than are available with poetry, both for speaking and for writing. It may even be that reading actually changes the minds of those who read. Such a distinction is possibly too fine for our purposes, because in the end, the results are the same. Reading somehow changes the way we think about and use language. Plato, standing on the shoulders of great thinkers before him, propagated the idea of knowledge as we now know it and established it as the proper study of an educational system, with these branches of study in classical antiquity: ethics, politics, psychology, physics, and metaphysics. Although Plato's student Aristotle brilliantly examined the subject of poetry in *The Poetics,* poetry, once the superior mode of discourse, lost the day to rational thought. The momentous shift from poetry's dominance as the sole kind of language to the preeminence of scientific thought had been accomplished. "Man's experience of his society, of himself, and of his environment was now given separate organized existence in the abstract word. . . . Europe still lives in their [Plato's and Aristotle's] shadow, using their language, accepting their dichotomies, and submitting to their discipline of the abstract as the chief vehicle of education, even to this day" (Havelock, 1963, 305).

Early Modern Consequences of Literacy

One might say that the principal consequence of the development of the alphabet and literacy was to change Western thinking, to provide a model of perceiving and using language, a model destined to penetrate every aspect of early modern Western literacy. It was many centuries, however, before the invention in Europe of movable type and the printing press in the fifteenth century A.D. released the full power of the alphabet. For hundreds of years after the invention of the Greek alphabet, literate Greeks, for the most part, copied down manuscripts of oral Greek literature, such as the Homeric epics and Athenian plays. How could it be otherwise? Rational language had not yet been conceived.

The Romans adapted the Greek alphabet for their own use and with their own symbols, and Roman literature flourished until roughly the fall of the Roman Empire at about the end of the fifth century A.D. After this time, Western literacy became a craft literacy, and only those whose primary function was to copy over existing manuscripts or to use language for written purposes, typically monks, priests, and others in religious orders, were able to read and write.

It was only the invention of movable type and the letterpress printing press, "the iron-and-levers-and-roller-based rude mechanicals that enabled all to enjoy and savor the teachings of the ancients" (Winchester, 2001, 8). The consequences of cheap and easy printing affected family life, communication, and education; it enabled the rapid expansion of libraries and other repositories of written language and the development of the English language and of modern science; and it even contributed to the concept of democracy in Great Britain, an idea that then spread to the American colonies and led to the creation of the United States.

A primary consequence of printing was its effect on family life. For the first time, the socialization of children—moral as well as educational—was removed from the family and handed over to persons who were not members of the children's immediate families. As we might imagine, this was a wrenching change. This practice grew until, in the nineteenth century, most of the children in Europe and in the United States who received schooling were in schools for "universal education, a profound and revolutionary move . . . The development of writing, then, involved the establishment of schools, the training of teachers [and] the emergence of specialist producers of knowledge" (Goody, 1999, 30,31).

And as a result of "book learning," schooling became longer and more abstract. Children's education grew longer because after a fairly extended period of learning to read and write, children then had to be at least exposed to the literary canon of the culture, including essays and other works written in this new expository, "scientific" prose. Instruction became more and more removed from "real life" and increasingly abstract, because pupils now learned about the world not at home or on the job but through books while squirming in classrooms. As we can appreciate from our present-day experiences in schools, education appeared to have little to do with the "real world." The chief complaint from students to this day is that school consists of sticking one's nose in books, listening to teachers lecture, and talking about impractical matters, rather than actually doing anything in the world "out there." The implication is that schooling has little relevance to their lives. And the student has only the invention of the alphabet and printing press and abstract language to thank for this brand of education.

The invention of printing also had a far-reaching effect on communications systems. We have only to look around us to see how completely the written word dominates our lives. Granted, a great deal of information is passed on to us orally through television, but even there, it is surprising how much of this information is either in print or is based upon print. In fact, we have been officially notified by the *New York Times* that, through what is known as the "Crawl" on cable news programs, "television has become a

print medium" (Sella, 2001, 66). Anyone who watches the major cable networks—CNN, Fox News, and MSNBC—cannot help but notice the continuous, scrolling information printed across the bottom of the TV screen. The reason for the Crawl, we are informed, is that with the glut of "breaking news," the cable new channels believe it is impossible to channel "through a single televised human" all the information from the events occurring throughout the world at this moment, and thus "the Crawl is multimedia's alternative to Babel." Possibly, though, the Crawl is a "favor to the younger generation of multitaskers." For others, the swiftly moving blurbs are, to say the least, distracting (Sella, 2001, 66).

Reading and writing also take up a great deal of time for literate people: in newspapers, in magazines, in mail—wanted or not—and on the computer, a technological invention that requires more, rather than less, reading and writing than ever before.

In addition, the invention of print has allowed us to accumulate and store information from all over the globe and from centuries long past. "As an agent of change, printing altered methods of data collection, storage, and retrieval systems and communication networks used by learned communities throughout Europe. It warrants special attention because it had special effects" (Eisenstein, 1979, xvi). Modern storage retrieval systems are marvelous developments. We are able to pull up past information in seconds, and we have the luxury—which we accept without thinking about it—of studying and analyzing printed information at our leisure and now, because of the computer, in our own homes. We can then skim and choose what material we wish to retain from the available print. Such an activity is impossible with oral language. "Documents give us a different sense of history, since we can readily retrieve the literature of our predecessors, their spoken word as well as their visual records" (Goody, 1999, 31).

Now, however, the storage system may be a victim of its own success. Our libraries, so administra-

tors report, are running out of room to store the plethora of printed matter produced in books, in periodicals, and especially in newspapers. Storing such materials on microfilm and microfiche has not solved the unanticipated and unwelcome problem. One interested "friend of the library," Nicholson Baker, in his aptly titled book *Double Fold: Libraries and the Assault on Paper* (2001), argues that there is no need for library officials to convert countless books and newspapers to microfilm, which in any case does not always preserve print, since often over years the print fades, develops spots and blemishes, and even suffers from fungal infections (Baker, 2001, cited in Gates, 2001, 8). Baker first spoke out in the San Francisco Library's auditorium in 1996 as a "library activist" against the library's practice of sending books to landfills because it had no room to store them. He also complains about the current library practice of "disbanding" books, in which librarians "guillotine" volumes—which had not been checked out for decades—along their spines and then throw them away. He feels so strongly about saving old newspapers, such as the *Chicago Tribune,* the *New York World,* and the *New York Times,* from destruction that he has started a nonprofit foundation for rescuing valuable old newspapers and is renting a decrepit warehouse in New Hampshire, where he stores thousands of volumes of old newspapers scheduled for destruction (Gates, 2001, 8). Some librarians say that they cannot stop destroying priceless books and newspapers. "We simply can't save everything," they exclaim, literally and figuratively throwing up their hands. But Baker replies, "Well, we're not asking them to save everything. We're not talking about airplane tickets or check stubs here. We're talking about the major newspapers that should be at the top of their lists of things to save" (Garner, 2001, 9).

Modern political bureaucracies also owe their existence to the alphabet and the invention of printing. Only with writing can we retain the information that forms the basis of all such organizations: files, cor-

respondence, and financial accounts as well as a country's evidence and records of all its interactions with other governments. Furthermore, no political bureaucracy can exist without legal codes, and writing drastically altered legal activities. Courts, in effect, began to depend on written records rather than on oral evidence and testimony for trials and other transactions. Written statutes and laws form the basis of a literate society. How can a legal system exist without lawyers and judges looking up what a previous ruling "said" for a precedent? Writing made it possible to save exact copies of contracts and laws rather than having lawyers rely on oral testimony. Even oral depositions and oral testimony are turned into written records to be later examined in solitude by lawyers and judges. No longer can a person orally lay claim to a title for owning land; written records of all titles have become the standard.

The invention of the alphabet and later the printing press also profoundly influenced the progress of the Protestant Reformation and, some believe, may have at the same time led to the birth of modern science. Printing, according to this view, had a direct influence on how literate individuals perceived Scripture and on how scientists viewed the natural world (Eisenstein, 1983; Olson, 1999).

This is a bold position indeed, but let us examine how it is substantiated. The basic argument is this: Printing "fixed"—providing large numbers of identical copies—both Scripture and ancient "science" books, which dealt with the natural world. These fixed, original, and objective texts were then put into millions of hands (Olson, 1991, 151). Print allowed a clear distinction between what was "observed" and the "interpretation" of what was seen as "fixed," "objective," and "permanent."

The core element of the religious movement of the sixteenth century in Europe was the "return to the book." Before the advent of printing, the Roman church's official view of interpretation was that expressed by Thomas Aquinas in his thirteenth-century *Summa Theologica:* Aquinas held that there are several levels of interpretation in Scripture, including literal, spiritual, and moral interpretations. All of these levels of meaning were inherent, "given," in the text.

Printing made an exact copy of Scripture available to anyone who could read and thus also made possible a new, personal way of interpreting the Bible. The Protestant reformer Martin Luther articulated the radically new viewpoint that there is a literal, historical meaning in the text of Scripture. Everything else attributed to Scripture, he held, is the result of tradition, of individuals attempting over time to "interpret" Scripture for those who were unlettered. Scripture—the exact, printed copy of the book—stands by itself, inviolate and autonomous, and needs no interpretation. All the rest is made up, a product of centuries of human explanation. If we accept this stance, we acknowledge the crucial distinction between the "given"—in this case, the "given" of the exact, faithful, printed copy of Scripture—and various "interpretations" of the everlasting, unchanging book made throughout the ages by literate theologians.

How did the invention of the printing press lead to the rise of modern science at the same time it was influencing theological thought? The connection between print and the interpretation of Scripture is analogous to the connection between print and a new interpretation of the natural world by early modern scientists, in which a special "scientific" language for observing the natural world, a "given," for writing about the meaning of these observations, "interpretation," is now available.

During the Middle Ages, it was common to speak of two kinds of "books": Scripture as God's word and nature as God's work (Olson, 1991, 154). Francis Bacon in 1620 wrote of "the book of God's word and the book of God's work" (quoted in Olson, 1991, 154). Thomas Browne, a seventeenth-century cleric, talked of God's two great books, Scripture and nature. To make this view slightly more complex, Galileo maintained that the book of nature was written in the lan-

guage of mathematics. Eric Havelock believes the modern scientific era did not depend solely on the printed page, important as it was "for the compilation and distribution of theoretic reasoning and empirical information"; he holds that "it relied also upon a revolution in the symbolization of quantitative measurement' (Havelock, 1976, 78). Musical "literacy," in this view, should be added to linguistic and numerical literacy, to complete the picture of the three literacies responsible for the modern era. "Linguistic, numerical, and musical 'literacy,' so to speak, can be thought of as forming a tripartite foundation of Western culture, built upon three technologies each of which is designed to trigger mental operations with automatic rapidity by using the sense of visual recognition" (Havelock, 1976, 81).

For those who created the modern scientific movement, the "given" of natural "facts"—analogous to the "given" word of Scripture—was the foundation upon which modern science was built. Everything else, the interpretation of nature, all the hypotheses, inferences, and "final causes," was invented by man. Even today, the nature of science is still founded on the distinction between "observation" and "inference." Observations of eternal nature are supposedly objective and reliable; inferences are made by humans and are merely theoretical interpretations of these observations. Although this distinction has undergone some revisions in modern times, present-day scientists still consistently and systematically separate observation from hypothesis. In short, centuries ago, reading the book of nature—that is, making scientific observations— was a new method for interpreting the facts of the natural world. This new science of interpretation, originally applied to Scripture, is hermeneutics, the science and methodology of interpretation.

In the process of creating a new way of viewing the natural world, print was also responsible for changing scientific language. Since scientists now read "perfect," exactly reproduced, printed books of observations and theoretical statements—what we now call primary sources—they had to devise a new language for writing about the book of nature. Early modern scientists could talk about novel ideas only if they coined new words to express these unfamiliar conceptions. For instance, early scientists arrived at such fundamental terms as 'observation" and "inference," "fact" and "theory," and "evidence" and "claim." The also made up a whole set of related concepts, such as "hypothesis," "conclusion," "conjecture," "assertion," and "assumption" (Olson, 1991, 155).

These early modern scientists also began to develop a new discourse for writing about science by writing not in the then-familiar flowery style but in a new, "plain" style. For instance, in 1667, the historian of the Royal Society of London, Thomas Sprat, described how members' writing should reflect the society's current attitudes toward Scripture and nature. The society was concerned "with the advancement of science and with the improvement of the English language as a medium of prose" and demanded a mathematical plainness in style, free from all "amplifications, digressions, and swellings of style" (quoted in Olson, 1991, 155–156).

In short, it very well may be that the great changes of this period in religion and science were direct results of new ways of thinking about Scripture and the natural world, and this new thinking in turn changed scientific prose:

> Perhaps Luther, Galileo and Descartes shared a common but new way of reading—of relating what was said to what was meant by it! But even to pose such questions required some analysis of just what scripts and writing systems are, how they relate to speech, how they are read, how those ways of reading changed, how ways of reading called for new distinctions, new awareness and new modes of thinking . . . how the very structure of knowledge was altered by the attempts to represent the world on paper. (Olson, 1994, xvii)

Finally, several scholars have focused on the influence of the printing press, via the publication

of a single book, the King James Bible of 1611, on the English language and on the birth of popular government both in England and in the American colonies.

First, what was the impact of the publication of the King James Bible on the English language itself? "Many of the Semitic turns of phrase that have gained an accepted place in modern English," we are told by Alister McGrath, "can be traced directly to the King James Bible of the old Testament" (2002, 362). McGrath quotes William Rosenau, from his 1978 book *Hebraisms in the Authorized Version of the Bible,* who stated flatly that the King James Bible "has been—it can be said without any fear of being charged with exaggeration—the most powerful factor in the history of English literature" (quoted in McGrath, 2002, 263).

Here are examples of Hebraic idioms that have become a part of English usage: "sour grapes," "pride goes before a fall," "to put words in his mouth," and "like a lamb to slaughter" (McGrath, 2002, 263). Other English phrases that have been adopted, with some minor changes, from Hebrew include these: "rise and shine," "to see the writing on the wall," "a fly in the ointment," and "a drop in the bucket" (McGrath, 2002, 264).

The case has also been made that printing the various translations of the Bible, and especially the King James Bible, was responsible for creating popular government, a novel and dangerous idea in both England and the American colonies in an era of kings and queens. As Simon Winchester reports in his review of both Alister McGrath's book *In the Beginning* and Benson Bobrick's book *Wide as the Waters,* Bobricks's "case is that the very warp and woof of popular government was created by the democratization of translated Scripture—that the newly evangelized people won from the Bible's teachings a spiritual strength sufficient to help them overcome the tyranny of their arrogant and detached rulers" (2001, 8). In the following quotation, Benson Bobrick presents his case for the unimaginable

power of the King James Bible to affect all aspects of the era:

> The growth of independent thought in the interpretation of the Bible was symptomatic of a larger spirit of questioning and inquiry which marked the age. Traditional explanations of the physical universe were rapidly yielding to the revelations of astronomy and the New Science, even as continued exploration of the globe "stimulated imagination in every walk of life." In politics, people began to insist on their right to a government that ruled with equity and justice, and in religion, on their right to worship as they pleased. Their [the general public's] free discussions about the authority of Church and state fostered concepts of constitutional government in England, which in turn were the indispensable prerequisites for the American colonial revolt. Without the vernacular Bible—and the English Bible in particular, through its impact on the reformation of English politics—there could not have been democracy as we know it, or even what today we call the "Free World." In short, the English Bible, with all that followed in its train, had sanctioned the right and capacity of the people to think for themselves. (2002, 268–269)

It does not really matter whether or not the newly printed Bible turned those who read it into Christians. What was important was that two ideas from the Bible formed the basis for popular government in the Western world: first, that each person was born with certain inalienable rights that could not be taken away, and second, that any government built upon this recognition was truly a government "by, for, and of the people" (Winchester, 2001, 8).

Summary

1   **Three Kinds of Writing: Logographic, Syllabic, and Alphabetic.** In order to comprehend the nature of literacy, we need to know the story of writing. For centuries, people engraved or wrote symbols to represent objects, creatures, and ideas. The logographic system of writing employs signs to stand for whole words. The syllabic system uses signs to represent syllables. Only the

alphabetic system uses letters of an alphabet to represent the meaningful sounds—its phonemes—of language.

2 **Conditions for an Efficient Writing System.** For writing to be efficient, it needs to meet these conditions: it must be comprehensive, unambiguous, and employ relatively few—twenty to thirty—symbols. Although the alphabet, based upon the Greek invention around 750 B.C., is the most efficient writing system ever devised, it is not a perfect one, with exceptions that make it less than ideal. Such a situation is known as the "residual ambiguity" of any written language. The alphabetic writing system, however, was not created without flaws. Rather it was invented to ensure that its written symbols would trigger the corresponding sounds in speech for readers.

For a writing system to produce universal literacy, though, a fourth condition is necessary: an education system teaching children how to read and write while they are young enough and their brains pliable enough to internalize the concept of written symbols corresponding to speech sounds.

3. **The Invention of the Printing Press Responsible for Universal Literary.** Although alphabetic writing was conceived some eight centuries B.C. in Greece, many more centuries would pass before the invention of movable type and the printing press provided for the full power of writing to be released throughout the Western world.

4. **Consequences of Alphabetic Writing and the Printing Press.** The consequences of the invention of the alphabet and the subsequent invention of movable type and the printing press literally shaped Western thought and culture.

5. **Two Modes of Thought: Poetic and Expository.** In a deeply fundamental way the poetic language of the oral Homeric epics and Athenian plays was superseded by a new prosaic language, dissem-

inated chiefly by the Greek philosopher Plato. Greek oral poetry was repetitive, rhythmic, imagistic, concrete, and didactic, all the mnemonic features contributing to the ability of persons to learn by heart oral works. The content of the epics and plays consisted of familiar stories of heroes who were directly involved in the basic customs of the culture. The epics and plays were didactic because their primary purpose was to teach the public and family laws to a pre-literate people.

Plato synthesized the thinking of the day with a new kind of language—one that was rational, expository, abstract, and scientific—a discourse in direct opposition to Homeric poetry. The person epitomizing this new way of thinking and of using language was the "philosopher-king," a kind of individual we might term as an intellectual—rather than a poet—one who is capable of and who has an overwhelming desire for abstract thinking.

6. **Invention of the Printing Press Affecting All Aspects of Western Civilization**. The full effects of the alphabet were not realized, however, until the arrival of movable type and the printing press in the fifteenth century by the German Johannes Gutenberg. When cheap and plentiful printed matter was available for literate persons, the consequences of print were momentous and universal, affecting all aspects of society: family life, education, mass communication, libraries and all other storage systems for print, bureaucracies, law, religion, science. Print was also responsible for introducing a concept of government originally created by the ancient Greeks, that of democratic government.

Glossary

alphabetic script—Writing or print in which symbols stand for phonemes, the smallest meaningful sounds of a language, rather than symbols representing objects and ideas or syllables.

articulators—Organs of speech that change sounds by moving parts of the mouth, including the lower lip, the tongue, and the uvula (the movable flap in the back of the mouth.)

consonant—A speech sound produced by partial or complete obstruction of the air stream, such as that represented by the letters p, r, w, and h.

craft literacy—Term applied to individuals like medieval scribes who copied over manuscripts in languages they did not understand, such as Irish scribes copying Latin scripts.

Cyrillic alphabet—Alphabet incorrectly attributed to Saint Cyril, a Christian missionary (826–885 A.D.), used for certain Slavic languages, such as Russian and Bulgarian.

diacritical mark—A mark such as the cedilla of the French "façade," the accent ague of the French "élite," and the tilde of the Spanish "cañon" that is added to a letter, indicating a special pronunciation.

glottis—The opening between the vocal cords at the upper part of the larynx, also known as the vocal bands.

grapheme—A letter or letter combination that represents the phoneme of a language, such as the graphemes c and s in the words "cite" and "sight" that represent the phoneme/s/ or the graphemes f and ph in "fish" and "photograph" that stand for the phoneme/f/.

hermeneutics—The science and methodology of interpretation, especially of Scripture.

logographic script—Writing in which a writen symbol (logograph or ideograph) stands for an individual word. For instance, the symbol 4 is read as "four" in English and as "quatre" in French.

pharynx—The section of the alimentary canal that runs from the mouth and nasal cavities to the larynx.

phoneme—The smallest unit of meaningful sound in a language, e.g. the sounds represented by the letter u in "run" and "pun" are identical phonemes. The letters "r" and "p" represent different phonemes. The letter "p" in the words "spin" and "pin," however, represents different sounds (phones), but since the sounds are not meaningfully different, they represent the same phoneme/p/.

points of articulation—Fixed parts of the mouth against which the movable articulators are placed to create various sounds. The points of articulation are the upper lip, upper teeth, alveolar ridge (the bony ridge toward the front of the roof of the mouth), palate (soft part of the upper mouth), and the velum (the back of the upper mouth, the soft palate.)

residual ambiguity, law of—The linguistic law that states no script ever provides a perfect correspondence between the signs of a language and the possible sounds they are designed to represent.

resonating cavities—Hollow chambers where speech sounds are created: the pharyngeal cavity (area in back of throat), nasal cavity (nose), and oral cavity (mouth).

Roman (or Latin) alphabet—The alphabet from which our modern English letters are derived. The original Roman alphabet, adopted from the Greek alphabet by way of the Etruscan alphabet, consisted of 23 letters, and was the basis for numerous scripts around the world, including those of modern western Europe.

syllabic script—Writing in which symbols represent not sounds (alphabetic script) or words (logographic script) but rather syllables.

trachea—Also caled the windpipe. A tube by which air is sent from the lungs through the pharynx, larynx, and the oral or nasal cavities and by which the sounds of language are produced.

unvocalized scripts—Scripts with consonants only, with no vowels, such as Hebrew.

unvoiced sound—A sound made with the vocal bands (glottis) open or unobstructed.

velar fricative—A sound made in the back of the tongue touching or near the soft palate as the "g" in "good" and the "k" in "king." The sound is not heard in modern English except in the Scottish "loch" meaning a lake."

vernacular—The native language of a country or locality. Also, the everyday language spoken by a people as distinguished by a learned or literary language. During the Middle Ages, the learned language was Latin while those in various countries spoke the vernacular, such as English, French, and German.

vocal bands—Also vocal cords. See glottis.

voiced sound—A sound made with the vocal bands (glottis) constructed or obstructed, such as the sounds represented by the letters "b" and "d."

vowel—A speech sound made by the relatively unobstructed passage of air through the larynx and oral cavity, usually forming the prominent and central sound of a syllable. In English the symbols for vowels are a, e, i, o, u and sometimes y.

CHAPTER THREE

How We Learned to Read

The technical changes in writing that occurred during the early Middle Ages, particularly the introduction of word separation and the development of encoded diacritical marks and signs of punctuation, affected the manner in which people read and thought. Each had discernible impact on the level and rapidity of cognitive activity, and each had potentially measurable implications for cerebral functions. The technical changes in book and document production that transpired between the years 1000 and 1500, when script was regularly separated and punctuated, had no major qualitative effects on cognition. Rather the use of the **vernacular** *and new book scripts of the late Middle Ages had its effect on the number of individuals who could participate in the private silent reading that the medieval restructuring of writing Latin engendered. Therefore, many of the changes, including the introduction of printing with movable type, that are detectable in books after 1200 constitute events more important for the history of literacy than for the history of reading.*

(Saenger, 1999)

vernacular

The native language of a people, as distinguished from a second academic or learned language, which for centuries in Europe was Latin.

How, over the centuries, have we developed mental strategies for finding meaning in the written or printed page? In other words, what goes on in my mind as I read? And how has this process changed over the millennia? Furthermore, has the appearance of the written page changed since ancient times, and if so how? And if it has changed, in what subtle and significant ways did it alter how I read? Very simply,

but not surprisingly, all these changes in language and writing have come about for one reason: to make reading easier. And we modern readers enjoy the advances in reading made over the centuries by legions of humble, unsung, dedicated scribes.

What We Do as We Read

We who are already fluent readers are unaware of these changes. For the most part, we know nothing of how language has changed and how the printed page looks to the eye lies below the level of conscious thought.

How has the radical change in reading occurred? Essentially, the appearance of the written page and later of the printed page—the "text format"—has been modified over the millennia. As the format of the page has evolved, so the structure of the language used in writing has also been transformed. As a result, our mental abilities have also evolved to keep pace with these changes.

When alphabetic writing was first invented, people from many cultures with varied languages used a variety of cognitive strategies to comprehend writing. No matter how many techniques we have employed over the centuries, however, there are two main elements of all written documents determining the cognitive processes we use to decode meaning from print: the structure of the language and the format of the written or printed page.

First is the arrangement of the parts of the language—its grammar and syntax. What syntax does the language exhibit? Does it show meaning by inflections—by word endings—as, for example, in ancient Greek, Latin, Old English, and modern German? Or does the syntax show meaning by word order and function words (e.g., articles, prepositions, and auxiliary words), as in modern English, whose most common sentence order is noun-verb-noun?

What do we mean by a language representing meaning by inflections? Take this simple Latin sentence, for instance:

Puer puellam amat.

If we ignore the Latin endings and just transcribe the words, one a time, into English words, keeping the word order, we have

Boy girl loves.

But if we now turn the sentence into English, that is, if we translate the inflected words in Latin, which uses word endings to convey meaning, into English, which, on the other hand, uses word order to convey meaning, we have

The boy loves the girl.

In Latin, we do not need to have English word order because Latin uses word endings to show meaning. The word *puer* stands for "boy," and since it is the subject of the sentence, it is in the nominative case and so does not have any special ending. The word *puellam,* "girl," is in the objective or accusative case, as is shown by the word ending *–am,* and is the object of the verb *amat.* The verb *amat,* we know from its inflection *–at,* is the third person singular form of the verb *amare,* "to love":

amo, "I love"
amas, "you love"
amat, "he, she, or it loves"

Also note that as we conjugate the verb *amare,* the word endings signify what in English is shown by the pronouns "I," "you," and "he, she, or it." Since English is not heavily inflected, we need the pronouns for meaning.

inflected language

A language, such as Latin, that conveys meaning by word endings, unlike an analytic language, like English, which conveys meaning chiefly by word order and function words.

Because both ancient Greek and Latin are **inflected languages**, the ancients wrote out their languages with the verbs frequently appearing last in sentences. Even with the simple sentence we have used as an example, we are obliged to read to the end of the sentence before we can tell what it

means. Imagine how difficult a long, complicated sentence with the verb at the end would be. Such a sentence is called "periodic," and it was a favorite grammatical construction for ancient writers. Common sense tells us and research has revealed that sentences in ordinary word order are much easier to read than are sentences with an inverted or unusual word order.

Vocabulary also determines how easy or hard a text is to read. What is the proportion of short, simple words to long, multisyllabic words in a piece of writing? Of ordinary, well-known words to specialized words that refer not to familiar objects and creatures but to abstract concepts? Do we immediately recognize these words as we read, or is it the first time we have met them? All such factors affect our ability to read.

Page format is the second major element determining difficulty or ease of reading. Again, we take for granted the modern printed page with all its graphic aids. What are some of these formatting features of modern print that make reading easy? Capitalization and punctuation, as well as paragraphing, running heads, bullets, outlining, marginal notes, and even page numbering—"**foliation**" or "pagination," as this practice is called—all help us to read more easily.

And of course, for effortless reading, we must included standardized spelling, known as "conventional **orthography**." We didn't begin to agree on common spellings for English words until the eighteenth century. Before that time writers spelled phonetically. For example, in the sixteenth and seventeenth centuries, Shakespeare spelled his own name several different ways. We finally agreed to spell English words uniformly, as always, to make reading easier.

Surprisingly, probably the most important feature of the written and printed page for making reading easier is the simple but profoundly important practice of leaving spaces between words. It is hard to imagine that the ancients first read writing

---

foliation

Numbering consecutively the leaves of a book or manuscript by Arabic numerals, now known as "pagination."

---

orthography

The art or study of correct spelling according to established usage, simply stated as standard, conventional spelling practices.

with no spaces, just continuous strings of printed letters. (**Cursive script** had not been invented yet.) Even for an especially trained, able, and conscientious elite, reading was slow and arduous, and those few who could read were forced to read out loud in order to make sense of frequently puzzling pages. All the aids to reading—the most important being word separation—were yet to be devised.

Recent scholarship has made an attempt "to explain the physiological influence of word separation on the reading process and to trace . . . the path of the adoption of word separation—the crucial element in the change to silent reading in medieval script" (Saenger, 1997, x).

> **cursive script**
> A form of writing, with successive lower case letters joined together, devised in the 1400s in Europe. In printing, cursive was a style that imitated handwriting.

How We First Read; Texts With No Word Separation

How did the ancients read texts in which the words—without capitals or periods of other marks of punctuation to show sentences and units within sentences—were all written together? Slowly and strenuously.

How was this process of reading script without word separation qualitatively different from modern reading? What psychological processes did ancient readers go through? As they read out loud, ancient readers had to keep their eyes ahead of their voice, so to speak, as they struggled to make sense of unseparated script. This process, so familiar to ancient Greeks and Romans, was thus a kind of "elaborate search pattern." They read by an incredibly complicated and sophisticated mental action in which the readers' eyes were constantly searching back and forth over strings of letters, unseparated and unpunctuated. As they scanned the letters, readers had to identify words by sounding out syllables and then by trying to figure out how they formed words—a complicated mental, visual probe, if you will.

As we know from contemporary research on the mental processes involved in reading, our eyes move across a page not in a steady, continuous rate but in

saccade

In reading, a rapid, intermittent eye movement across a page, not at a steady, continuous rate, but in a series of "leaps" or "jumps."

a series of "fixations" and "jumps," called "**saccades**." Just think how taxing the mental effort must have been for ancient readers. They had to make sense of unseparated scripts without the luxury of having words isolated from strings of letters and without the additional help of our modern graphic devices. We can only assume that the ancient reader expended much more mental energy than we do in processing all kinds of print.

Not only did the ancient readers need to scan the unseparated writing *forward* to search for words, they also had to look *backward*—making what are called "**ocular regressions**"—in order to make certain that the words they found did indeed contribute to the overall meaning of a sentence. Only rarely do we read today by ocular regressions. Obviously, there is no need for contemporary readers to make sure they have correctly separated words. But sometimes modern readers, who are skimming print, move so fast across the page that they make mistakes. As they continue reading, they realize that a previously scanned word does not make sense in the sentence being read, so they must reread it. For ancient readers, ocular regression must have been a common mental act. For the most part, this is not the case today.

ocular regression

The act of scanning the letters backward—as well as forward—in order to make certain that the words found do indeed contribute to the overall meaning of a sentence.

What other barriers did the unseparated script erect for the ancients? Since they read by sounding out a script syllable by syllable, they were able to process visually only a few chunks of letters at a time. Because of this radically reduced field of vision, with a great many more fixations and saccades, the ancients were forced to read very slowly. Instead of keeping one, two, or even three words in their minds, as we are able to do with modern separated texts—especially on a topic we are already familiar with—they could remember only a few syllables or at best short words, which in turn, they needed continually to identify and verify what they had just read. Imagine how very difficult it would have been for ancient readers to process current expository texts—with novel ideas and words—in this fashion.

Still other factors made reading unseparated text an arduous task for ancient readers. Not only did they have to pick out words from continuous strings of letters, they also had to deal with grammar or punctuation that we would find awkward and frequently puzzling (and often by today's criteria "incorrect"). For instance, ancient writers might join two declarative sentences without a conjunction of any mark of punctuation—called "**parataxis**"—as in the clauses "It was hot we remained in shade."

Another syntactical problem was that the ancients—apparently for rhetorical purposes—frequently used **periodic sentences**, those with verbs coming at the end. Placing the verbs in this position meant that readers had to wait until they had finished the sentence before they could grasp its meaning, moving back and forth through the strings of unseparated letters before the overall meaning of the sentence revealed itself.

Furthermore, as the ancients read this unseparated script, they had to do a kind of "prereading," called *praelectio*, an initial preparation before they read "for real." By first reading a text out loud, ancient readers kept in their minds those fragments that might be confusing until they had worked their way through complete sentences and were confident they understood them.

Some ancients reported they read not exactly silently but with a suppressed, muffled voice so they could enjoy privacy or concentrate on understanding the text. "Saint Augustine suggests that Ambrose read silently either to seek privacy by concealing the content of his book or to rest his voice." Nevertheless, "no classical author described rapid, silent reference consultation as it exists in the modern world. For the ancients, *lectio*, the synthetic combination of letters to form syllables and syllables to form words, of necessity preceded *narratio*, that is, the comprehension of a text" (Saenger, 1997, 8, 9).

If reading continuous letters out loud made reading such a painfully slow act, why did it take so long for writers to make reading easier by leaving

parataxis

Writing together clauses and phrases without coordinating or subordinating conjunctions, for example: "It was hot we felt roasted."

periodic sentence

A sentence construction in which the main clause or the verb comes at the end.

praelectio

For texts with no spaces between words, the ancient practice of "prereading" out loud, an initial survey of the text.

lectio

The Latin term for the practice by ancients of conducting a preliminary examination of a text with unseparated letters forming syllables and syllables forming words that preceded the actual comprehension of a text.

narratio

For ancient readers, this term meant "to comprehend a text," from the Latin *narrare*, *gnarus*, "knowing, to know."

spaces between words? There are several reasons why the ancients kept **scriptura continua.**

First, we need to keep in mind that the continued use of *scriptura continua* was possible only with an alphabetic script, with letters for both vowels and consonants making up a fairly complete set of symbols for transcribing the sounds of a language. Before vowels were added to consonants in the Greek script, "all the ancient languages of the Mediterranean world—syllabic or alphabetic, Semitic, or Indo-European—were written with word separation by either spaces or "points" (called "interpuncts," these dots were used throughout the Middle Ages to show syllable separation), or both in conjunction. After the introduction of vowels, word separation was no longer necessary to eliminate an unacceptable level of ambiguity (Saenger, 1997, 9).

In short, once vowels were added to the Greek script, writers felt no need to separate words by spaces. As they added vowels to scripts with consonants only to *scriptura continua,* scribes were no longer obligated to separate words. If ancient scripts had been written in consonants alone with all letters strung together without spaces, the scripts would have been nearly impossible to read.

A puzzling question remains. Some ancient writers added symbols for vowels to the consonants so that readers could make sense of unseparated script. In scripts for other languages with consonants only, such as Hebrew, scripts were written with word separation. Why didn't some ingenious scribe simply compose a script with symbols for both consonants and vowels and word separation all at the same time?

The answer cannot be that scribes in one language were unaware of how language was transcribed in another because recovered fragments of ancient writing show that Greeks, Romans, and Jews were all aware of each other's writing. Why then were the two systems not combined? We can only guess at the reasons, but it seems that the ancients had a cultural view toward reading and writing that we now find incomprehensible. First, the ancients showed no desire to make reading easier because few "reference texts," such as theological and scientific books, had yet been created. Even though the ancients had access to the writings of Plato and Aristotle, for the most part, they read relatively few literary texts, which they had read many times and knew by heart; they were not novel texts with new ideas, and therefore could be read slowly and savored. Thus, there was no need to copy such familiar text in unseparated script.

Moreover, it may be the ancients felt no need for a separated text because the idea that many people should become literate did not occur to them. There was no movement for universal literacy in the ancient world. Besides, professional readers—educated scribes who were often slaves—did virtually all the reading for their masters anyway. "It is in the context of a society with an abundant supply of cheap, intellectually skilled labor that attitudes must be comprehended and the ready and pervasive acceptance of the suppression of word separation throughout the Roman Empire understood" (Saenger, 1997, 11–12).

> The importance of word separation by space is unquestionable, for it freed the intellectual faculties of the reader, permitting all texts to be read silently, that is, with the eyes alone. As a consequence, even readers of modest intellectual capacity could read more swiftly, and they could understand an increasing number of inherently more difficult texts. Word separation also allowed for an immediate oral reading of texts, which eliminated the need for the arduous process of the ancient *praelectio*. Word separation, by altering the neuro-physiological process of reading, simplified the act of reading, enabling both the medieval and modern reader to receive silently and simultaneously the text and encoded information that facilitates both comprehension and oral performance. (Saenger, 1997, 13)

The Birth and Evolution of Modern Reading

For some nine hundred years after the fall of Rome, written texts continued to be copied without

word separation or marks of punctuation in *scriptura continua*. The task of separating words within strings of letters fell to the readers, not to the scribes. The readers had to read out loud, moving forward and backward along a line of printed letters, sounding out syllables, picking out words made up of these syllables, and then testing the words, still out loud, as to their meaning, and finally checking to see whether or not the words fit into the overall sense of a sentence.

And what were these basic changes in reading that occurred between ancient and early modern times? We went from reading scripts of unseparated letters to scripts in which there were spaces beween words. We went from reading scripts with no graphic aids to reading scripts with all the present-day aids to reading—punctuation marks, paragraphing, tables of contents, indexes, glossaries, and page numbering, to name a few—enjoyed by modern readers. As a result of these technical innovations, we went from reading out loud slowly and in a tiresome manner to reading silently, quickly, and most of the time, almost effortlessly. We went from a time when only scholastics and some of those in religious orders could read to one in which laypersons, beginning first with royalty, nobles, and wealthy urban leaders, could read. Finally, we went from reading Latin only to reading in the vernacular languages of Europe.

What historical processes caused these dramatic changes in how we read, and how did this transformation alter the cognitive processes needed to call forth meaning from writing or print?

The first impetus for this change was the trouble Irish scribes in the seventh century, who were copying Latin manuscripts, evidently had in reading the Gospels in classical Latin *scriptura continua*. The scribes were Celts, to whom Latin, the native tongue of Roman scribes, was a foreign language. How did these Irish scribes revise this strange writing—of supremely precious Scripture—to make it easier to read for those who found Latin foreign and difficult?

The Irish scribes noticed that in the Syriac Gospels they were copying, there were spaces between words, and they imitated this format in their work. They, and the Anglo-Saxon scribes they trained, realized that if they separated words, readers would no longer need to read out loud to make sense of what they read.

In short, "the postancient period of the history of reading and script began in Ireland and England at the end of the seventh century when Celtic monks, for whom Latin was a foreign tongue . . . introduced word separation and syntactic punctuation (i.e., punctuation that isolated units of meaning) into Latin and Greek texts" (Saenger, 1999, 12).

Not only did the scribes begin to use word separation, but they also developed a process of writing comments between the lines of Latin script. These interlinear notes now made it possible to understand complicated and ambiguous Latin sentences without reading out loud. The scribes found this new script so successful that they immediately used it for a new kind of prayer book, one intended for those who could read it silently and in privacy. This separated script, though, little known outside the British Isles and Brittany—on the coast of what is now France—and in some insulated Celtic and Anglo-Saxon monastic colonies, remained isolated for some three centuries.

Reading at the Beginning of the Early Modern Era

Although the idea of separating continuous strings of letters into words and using punctuation to isolate units of meaning began in the seventh century in Ireland, it was restricted to Ireland and southern England for some three hundred years. Not until the tenth century do we find evidence of word-separated scripts in the writings of monks in France and Switzerland. In the beginning of the thirteenth century, this new script was used in England, northern France, and in Germany, and it later came to be used in southern France, Italy, and Spain. After centuries of changes in the format of ancient Latin *scriptura continua,* w could finally read silently, pri-

vately, and easily. This script now allowed us to read complex treatises and books on theology, philosophy, and science.

> By the thirteenth century, all of western Europe, from Scotland and Denmark in the north to Spain and Italy in the south, had adopted a single and generally homogeneous form of written Latin that incorporated both the graphic conventions of canonical separation and the principles of word order and syntactic word grouping. This new Latin, which was so different from the Latin of antiquity, became the medium of intellectual discourse for scholars. It was a medium with minimal ambiguity, compared with the writing system that had preceded it. (Saenger, 1997, 256)

The general adoption of the new word-separated script transformed all aspects of literacy. The script radically changed the way university students were taught to read, the physical nature of libraries, the rise of heretical thoughts, and the development of texts in languages other than Latin—in vernacular languages such as Italian, French, German, and English. Word-separated script contributed to the rise of humanism, first in Italy and then throughout the rest of Europe, and because of an increase in private, silent reading, it allowed for the rapid spread of individual, personal thought and expression.

quire

A set of twenty-four or sometimes twenty-five leaves of four, double sheets of parchment or paper of the same size or stock, folded one within another in a manuscript or book.

gloss

A brief, explanatory note and sometimes translated foreign term or unusual technical term, either in the margins or between the lines of a text.

These changes in scripts did not allow just for the expression of new ideas. They also changed the physical act of writing itself. Ancient authors had written on waxed tablets and papyrus. Now scholars composed on **quires**—sets of usually twenty-four sheets of parchment—and writers enjoyed a much less taxing mode of composition. They now could revise what they had written, move sections around on separate sheets of parchment, and refer to ideas from other sheets. Because parchment came in sheets, readers could move back and forth from one argument to another without going through a whole scroll or searching individual waxed tablets to find a particular passage. During the thirteenth century, authors began to write notes—**glosses** and commentaries—in the margins of manuscripts. Writing on

tablets was slow, hard work. In reaction to this practice, scribes and authors developed a looped script physically easier to do than was the old manner of printing by hand, and so cursive was born.

The following quotation from Umberto Eco's novel *The Name of the Rose* provides a delightful description of the work of scribes during the fourteenth century. In this case, a scribe copies "the pages of a richly illuminated psalter":

> The [pages] were folios of the finest vellum—that queen among parchments—and the last was still fixed to the desk. Just scraped with pumice stone and softened with chalk, it had been smoothed with the plane, and, from the tiny holes made on the sides with a fine stylus, all the lines that were to have guided the artist's hand had been traced. The first half had already been covered with writing, and the monk had begun to sketch the illustrations in the margins. The other pages, on the contrary, were already finished, and as we looked at them, neither I nor William could suppress a cry of wonder. (Eco, 1994, 76)

Not only was the traditional Latin script *textualis* unsuited for expressing abstract statements, but printing it by hand in a **codex** was just plain hard work. In **illuminations**—miniature pictures in the books of the time—we see scribes printing books in what looks to be a physically demanding way. Early illuminations show scribes with quill in one hand and a knife in the other. Writers used the knife to sharpen their quills, but they also used the arm with the knife to balance the writing hand. The hand with the knife also held the parchment firmly in place while the scribes printed the traditional *textualis*. The new way of writing was essentially the way we write today. Medieval illuminations show writers—just like us except for dress, robes, and cowls—holding a parchment in place with one hand while writing a flowing, cursive script with the other.

Because of word-separated writing, scribes and scholars could now copy and compose silently and in delicious privacy. They no longer needed to read out loud while printing with the help of other

textualis

An ancient script of formal Latin, used almost exclusively for copying manuscripts and books in the form of *codices*.

codex

A manuscript volume, first used by the early Christians in the first century A.D. for the Scriptures used in their liturgy. One could write on both sides of the parchment pages of codex but on only one side of a papyrus scroll, and a codex was easier to read and handle than a scroll. By the early second century A.D. all Scripture was copied in codex form.

illumination

The art of hand-decorating a text, page, or initial with beautiful, full-colored designs, miniature pictures, or lettering.

scribes. Solitary authors, now writing in a strikingly user-friendly script, could move back and forth from one quire to another, for the first time getting a sense of an entire manuscript. They could make cross-references throughout their writing, adding supplements, and finally revising an overall manuscript before submitting it for publication to scribes in a *scriptorium*.

The new cursive, word-separated script also led to significant changes in methods of instruction in the medieval university classroom. We need to note that the educational practices described here dealt almost exclusively with teaching university students and those in religious orders how to read and write. Although some persons were taught to read by private tutors, all others became literate in university classrooms or in religious environments.

In the late medieval period, we first observe a university teaching method that has persisted for centuries: a professor reads from a textbook while students follow identical texts of their own. Even though more and more academics and their students began to read silently in private, the public lecture was the primary method of teaching. What were the results of such a practice? There was the usual problem of students who failed to bring their texts to class. To resolve this dilemma, universities required students, by statute, to bring their texts to class. In 1259, for instance, the Dominican house of the University of Paris insisted that students come to class with copies of the text the professor was explicating. The lecture method was also adopted for public worship, and "collective prayer could be enriched by individuals gazing on the text of a written prayer as it was collectively pronounced" (Saenger, 1997, 259). Here again is another modern practice for both university classrooms and churches, first started in the Middle Ages.

What were poor students to do if they could not afford personal copies of texts? They did basically what poor students do today. In what may have been the beginning of student aid, students too

poor to buy their own texts were allowed to borrow them from libraries, such as that of the Cathedral of Notre Dame in Paris. Benefactors made contributions to help defray the costs of stocking libraries with multiple copies of texts for poor students. (Could this have been the creation of charitable bequests to educational institutions?) At this time, universities also came up with a solution to another problem still faced by university libraries: ensuring that students returned their borrowed books. "The statutes of the Sorbonne [in Paris] provided for lending books against security deposits" (Saenger, 1997, 259).

Those who wrote these new works and copied old ones introduced other features of text format. Not only did authors and perceptive scribes divide books into chapters and break up chapters into more easily manageable parts, called **distinctiones**, but they also devised such further aids to reading as chapter headings, lists of subjects arranged alphabetically, and the titles of texts or of chapters on every page of a sheet of parchment, now known by printers as "running heads" or "running titles."

distinctiones
Latin term for logically dividing chapters and further divisions of chapters into separate parts.

From the thirteenth century on, scribes began to use a new kind of punctuation, the colored paragraph mark, which pointed out various intellectual units. "Illuminated capitals were employed in the fourteenth century to help clarify the new sequential argumentation in the fashion of *ad primum, ad secundum,* and so on" (Saenger, 1997, 260).

These imaginative scholars and scribes also added brief explanatory notes and sometimes translated foreign words or puzzling technical terms, either in the margins or between the lines of a text. The helpful additions, called "glosses," are still in use today, especially in specialized technical textbooks. A list of such words, arranged alphabetically, we know as a "glossary."

All these changes and additions to the format of the written page were devised to aid the late medieval reader as he read, silently and privately, complex translations of old books and many complicated new books. "The complex structure of the written

page of a fourteenth century text presupposed a reader who read only with his eyes, going swiftly from objection to response, from table of contents to the text, from diagram to the text, and from the text to the gloss and its corrections" (Saenger, 1997, 260). Without word separation and all the typographical devices we have noted, the development and dissemination of new knowledge that occurred from this time on would have proceeded at a much slower pace or might not have happened at all.

How were medieval texts produced before the invention of the printing press? By the thirteenth and fourteenth centuries, the **pecia** system was in place, in which professional scribes were employed to turn out "correct," very legible copies of all of the standard texts used throughout the university curriculum. It is recorded, for example, that the scribes at the University of Angers could finish an acceptable copy of a text within a month for a fairly reasonable price. University "**stationers**"—as medieval publishers and booksellers were called—rented standard copies of textbooks to students and guaranteed the quality of the exemplary texts. Once the printing press was instituted, of course, the problem of making identical texts available to university students was solved. And so the modern university bookstore was born.

> Not only were these textbooks with their gradually developed reader-friendly page formats necessary for students to understand the intricacies of public lectures, but books with such formats became indispensable for private reading, now an accepted part of university life. Paintings and illuminations of the fourteenth and fifteenth centuries in vernacular books intended for the lay reader showed motionless scholars reading in libraries, both in groups and in isolation, with their lips sealed, an unmistakable **iconographic** statement of silence. Inexpensive Latin and vernacular compendia of large treatises became popular to serve the growing student need for private study. (Saenger, 1997, 261)

Changes in reading, as we might expect, brought about significant physical changes in libraries (includ-

pecia
Medieval practice in which professional scribes produced "correct" copies of standard texts, used throughout a university curriculum.

stationer
Medieval publisher and bookseller.

iconographic
A set of related pictorial illustrations of a particular subject. Exquisite pictures in medieval manuscripts revealed the lives of well-known persons and activities of the time.

ing the introduction of special furniture) and in the ways in which these libraries were used. What were libraries like before the invention of word-separated reading? In ancient libraries, within secluded convents and monasteries, almost all the time everyone read out loud. Those persons who did study by themselves in cloisters and carrels, which were isolated by stone walls, were able to read softly to themselves in low voices or dictate to secretaries without disturbing their neighbors. By the end of the thirteenth century, however, library architecture and even furniture had been dramatically altered to accommodate silent reading.

Reference texts were chained to the desks because they were valuable, one-of-a-kind works. Reference texts included such books as alphabetical dictionaries and "concordances"—alphabetic indices of words in a text or body of texts, showing occurrences of particular words. Other standard reference books were the books of Thomas Aquinas, biblical commentaries, and other works frequently cited by scholars. The statutes published by libraries of the time stated that books were to be chained to desks so all could refer to them: they existed for the common good. The secured reference books of the late Middle Ages were forerunners of another feature of modern libraries: the precious reference collection. In present-day libraries, reference works do not circulate. Rather, reference materials—now including such items as microfilm and microfiche—are open and available to all. Was the practice of keeping references for common use the beginning of free public libraries?

But the new physical spaces for silent reading in libraries, places of near-absolute silence, meant that patrons could no longer read out loud. At Oxford University in England, for instance, the regulations of 1412 stated that the library was a place of quiet. The rules of the library of the University of Angers in 1431 prohibited all talking, even "conversation and murmuring." By the fifteenth century, the rules laid down by the Sorbonne library, which had been in effect for decades, "proclaimed the chained library

of the college to be an august and sacred place, where silence should prevail" (Saenger, 1997, 263).

As the physical design of libraries was transformed by the silent reading, scribes devised new reference tools, such as catalogs with the names of authors arranged alphabetically. From the eleventh century on, scribes and **rubricators**, under the supervision of specially designated scholars, "corrected" previously written manuscripts by adding *prosodiae*, accepted punctuation marks. The job of professional rubricators was to provide rules or short commentaries in a book. A "rubric" (from the Latin word *rubrica*, "red earth, red ocher," from *ruber*, "red") later referred to the practice of coloring a title, a heading, or even an initial letter of a book section in red. Eventually, a rubric became the label for any authoritative rule written in red.

Just as modern students underline words, sentences, and passages or use markers to highlight passages, write notes in the margins of texts, and use all sorts of figures—lines, arrows, crosses, asterisks—to note important items, so readers in the late medieval period wrote phrases, idiosyncratic symbols, and assorted doodles in books. Early readers were apparently as bothered as we are by books with notations by former readers: Late medieval universities ruled that critical editing—"emendations"—should not be done by students and should be the same in all standard books. Scholarly works follow the same practice today by publishing "authorized" editions of texts.

In an amazing fashion, private, silent reading made possible, in an age of intellectual conformity, the spread of independent thought, especially of opinions or doctrines at odds with accepted religious beliefs and political doctrines of the day. "The transition to silent reading and composition, by providing a new dimension of privacy, had even more profound ramifications for both the lay and scholastic culture of the late Middle Ages. Psychologically, silent reading emboldened the reader because it placed the source of his curiosity

rubricator

In the eleventh century, scribes and rubricators corrected previously written manuscripts by adding accepted punctuation marks, known as *prosodiae*.

completely under personal control" (Saenger, 1997, 264).

During the ninth century, when most reading was done out loud, it was hard to make heretical thoughts public. Since authors dictated their ideas and presented them in public lectures—*lectios*—religious and political orthodoxy could be effectively maintained. But just two centuries later, in the eleventh century, those who read in seclusion were often accused of heresy. Since readers could now read privately, new speculations, especially subversive ideas in "tracts"—papers or pamphlets making appeals by representatives of religious or political groups—were not subject to censorship by the group. "Private, visual reading and private composition thus encouraged individual critical thinking and contributed ultimately to the development of skepticism and intellectual heresy" (Saenger, 1997, 264).

University professors, ever conscious of their right to free expression, knew that students could read writings of unacceptable ideas privately and outside the lecture hall because we have records from the thirteenth century of university statutes forbidding attendance by students at public readings of heretical books. In the fourteenth century-censorship of books, including book burning, was common. In 1323, for instance, the general chapter of the Dominican Order decreed that all books on alchemy—the ancient chemical philosophy that had as its aim the conversion of base metals into gold—were to be burned. Some prohibited books, however, were officially allowed to exist, primarily so theologians could prove them false.

What was the effect of this new script, first developed and used exclusively by those in religious orders and in universities, on the reading habits of laypersons? It took centuries before laypersons moved from reading orally to reading silently and from reading Latin texts to reading books written in the vernacular languages of Europe.

But during the late Middle Ages, momentous changes in vernacular texts occurred. Whereas once

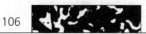

only ecclesiastics and academics read, now laymen, such as kings, nobles, and aristocrats, read. Reading practices changed from oral reading in groups to silent, private reading. Reading matter expanded from a body of well-known theological and philosophical texts to include new scientific works. Writing changed from printing to cursive script. The format of reading materials changed from pages with few reading aids to pages with such modern graphic aids as paragraphing, punctuation marks, standardized spelling, and even underlining (which in modern print is shown by italics). And as the changes in print were made more available, terms were devised to describe and talk about these new ways of presenting print. "The transformation from an early medieval oral, monastic culture to a visual scholastic one had at first only a limited effect on the reading habits of lay society, particularly in northern Europe, where oral reading and dictation of vernacular texts were commonly practiced at least until the thirteenth century" (Saenger, 1997, 265).

Why did silent reading by laypersons lag behind silent reading by academics or religious persons? Until the mid-fourteenth century, French kings and nobles had no reason to learn to read. They had scribes who did all their reading for them. When a prince like Saint Louis did read orally, he commonly read aloud as a member of a small group.

What did the royalty and the nobility read? Although they dutifully studied liturgical works, for the most part they read histories, verse, and long narrative poems rather than the newly created scholastic, philosophical, and scientific texts. We might suppose this was so because the laymen knew the poetic epics by heart and enjoyed reading them over time and again. These laymen read historical accounts—chronicles, that is, events arranged chronologically—of their countries. The read romances and **chansons de geste**, epic poems recounting the adventures of heroic characters, and the verse of the troubadours, poets popular in northern France during the twelfth and thirteen centuries. Most of the

chanson de geste

Any one of some eighty Old French epic poems written from the eleventh through the fourteenth century, celebrating the deeds of historical or legendary heroes, especially the adventures of Charlemagne.

works written in verse were intended for oral recitation as court performances. The *Roman du Lancelot,* for instance, and the *Histoire ancienne jusqu'a César,* an account of ancient history up until the reign of Caesar, were composed to be read aloud for kings and noblemen. Even at this time, "much of medieval vernacular poetry and prose was composed, memorized and performed orally and only later set down in writing" (Saenger, 1997, 266).

Because the first vernacular texts were meant for listeners rather than for silent readers, the tradition of composing vernacular texts by dictation and the development of cursive writing fell behind the use of cursive for scholastic texts. Even during the thirteenth century, when scholastic scribes employed cursive script on unbound sheets and quires, vernacular texts were still being written in the traditional *textualis,* the time-honored, hand-printed script used over centuries for copying medieval manuscript books.

Eventually, after many years, the scribes who did copy down vernacular texts began to use the techniques they had acquired copying word-separated, medieval Latin texts. Incorporating the new aids to reading, the scribes gradually brought about changes in vernacular texts; most importantly, they spelled words more consistently and with a practice that changed the nature of modern languages, scribes dropped word inflections and introduced natural word order in sentences. The scribes changed the structure of written Old English, for example, from a heavily inflected language to that of Early Modern English, an **analytic language**, in which meanings were conveyed by word order and function words.

Not only were words in the vernacular now spelled more uniformly, but they were also spelled less phonetically than they had been in Latin. What did this have to do with reading? When words were spelled uniformly rather than phonetically, and once readers of vernacular script saw a new word and heard it pronounced, they could immediately recog-

---

analytic language

A language, like English, that uses word order and function words—unlike a heavily inflected language like Latin, that uses word endings—to show meaning.

nize it when they saw it again—instead of sounding out phonetically different spellings of the same word—and they were able to read it from then on without trouble.

Only at the beginning of the fourteenth century did scribes, using Gothic cursive script along with an accepted word-separated text format, first begin to transcribe vernacular texts. At the same time, illiterate princes of France evidently realized that their realms had become so large and complex that they needed to keep records and communicate in writing with other princes in order to manage their estates. This meant they must now learn to read and write. It was no longer appropriate for royalty to rely on professional readers, as they had before, and kings started a custom that persists to this day of having secretaries write out draft letters and official documents in cursive vernacular. The kings would then edit the documents before signing them. One such forward-looking chief operating officer, Charles V of France, made corrections to drafts of letters and then signed edited copies. We have evidence that a century later, certain official letters were written by the kings themselves, and frequently letters from kings bore the royal "autograph signature."

It was not until the mid-fourteenth century that French nobility finally began to accept the custom of silent reading and the use of cursive writing. During his reign, John II was responsible for having a great deal of Latin literature translated into vernacular French. This effort was successful because the scribes translating Latin into French now had before them examples of recent scholastic texts with a syntax that, unlike that of the difficult ancient Latin texts, was much closer to the word order of the contemporary vernacular.

Other French kings continued to support reading and writing in the language of their people. Charles V, after the death of John II, carried on his work by ordering more translations of vernacular books. Charles V has the distinction of being the first king to establish a royal library, fittingly enough in

a tower of the Louvre, with furniture like that found in university libraries. Illustrators painted miniatures of King Charles "seated in his library, motionless, not declaiming, reading with sealed lips in silent and tranquil isolation. Manuscripts also depicted the king attending lectures, visually following a copy of the text in the university fashion as he listened to the lecture" (Saenger, 1997, 268).

Along with reading vernacular texts silently went a new precise vocabulary to describe these innovations. In the Middle Ages before silent reading, monks had used the term **in silentio** to describe how they read their Latin texts orally: in a low, muffled voice, also called *submissa vox* or *suppressa vox*. "In the fifteen century, vernacular authors employed a new, explicit vocabulary of silent reading, describing mental devotion from a written text as reading with the heart, as opposed to the mouth" (Saenger, 1997, 268). French aristocratic texts employed the phrase **lire au coeur**, "reading from the heart," to designate private, silent reading.

Now that royals and nobles had learned to read vernacular texts and found they liked reading, they hungered for more and more books to read. Because of private, silent reading, vernacular books changed from traditional treatises and literary texts to newly created books "almost exclusively in prose." "French authors composed for the nobility new reference books, including alphabetical dictionaries of saints and gazetteers" (Saenger, 1997, 269). And as the types of books being read changed, the format of the new vernacular prose books also changed. Scholars and other authors added to them all the features of page layout that had already become common in the scholastic books of the thirteenth, fourteenth, and fifteenth centuries: tables of contents, alphabetically arranged glossaries, subject indexes, and running heads. Authors now agreed more and more on standard spelling of words, and as a result, this period may have seen the beginning of teaching reading by word recognition. By this time, words were separated and were spelled in a fairly consistent

---

in silentio

In the Middle Ages, before persons learned to read silently and in private, this term was used to instruct monks and others how to read texts orally in a low, muffled voice.

---

lire au coeur

A phrase for reading silently and in private, meaning literally "to read from the heart," rather than out loud, from the mouth.

way, so once readers learned a word, they did not have to sound it out over and over again when they encountered a new spelling of it. They now were familiar with the word and read it without hesitation. In these new vernacular texts, "orthography became increasingly standardized, enabling the reader to recognize words by their global image, as in Latin, rather than to decode them phonetically by an ad hoc synthetic combination of phonemes" (Saenger, 1997, 269).

This was also a time of illustrating books, of painting pictures and miniatures as teaching devices to help lay readers understand prose texts. This practice was a logical extension of the scholastic technique of using diagrams to explain unfamiliar academic and theological texts. Authors also transferred another visual aid from scholastic to vernacular texts, called **banderoles**, ribbon-shaped figures written in the margins of books and containing useful information; this was another contrivance to help readers understand the prose they encountered. All these graphic aids—paragraphing, illustrations, miniatures, banderoles, illuminated letters (many times stories in themselves)—look comfortably like the modern reading aids we accept without question, such as magazine and book illustrations, photographs, and computer-generated visual aids. Only in some scholarly books do we still find page after page of long paragraphs uninterrupted by pictures, diagrams, or illustrations.

Before the 1300s, when professional readers read to kings and nobles, books were composed in *textualis,* the traditional script formerly used exclusively in copying Latin manuscript books. This was acceptable because university readers were familiar with this writing. As we might imagine, when laypersons began to read in the vernacular for the first time, they found *textualis* too hard for them. One particular barrier to comprehension was the practice in *textualis* of printing all letters in lowercase figures and of writing the letters "m," "n," "i," and "u" in the identical, vertical "minim" strokes

banderole

A ribbon-shaped figure written in the margin of a book, containing added useful information.

The scribes, aiming to please the lay readers for this new reading market in the last twenty years of the fourteenth century, created a "new, improved" script, written rather than printed, called *cursiva formata*. In the first half of the fifteenth century, the authors and scribes came up with a new version of *cursive formata*. Because this advanced script was written in cursive but was still part *textualis,* it was called **lettre batarde**, "bastard script." Modern scholars, who cannot pinpoint the precise date and place of this invention, identify this type of writing by a more polite name, *hybrida,* "hybrid" script. So successful was *lettre batarde* or *hybrida* that authors and scribes began to use it for transcribing Latin as well as for copying vernacular texts. It is interesting to note that until this time, all the innovations in vernacular scripts were copied from scholastic, Latin writing. However, with the appearance of *hybrida,* we find, for the first time, vernacular writing influencing academic writing.

lettre batarde

Known as the "bastard script" because it evolved as a combination of an earlier Gothic *textualis*, which was difficult to read, and an existing cursive script, *cursiva formata*.

Laypersons, who might be able to pronounce words in Latin texts phonetically without understanding them, could now read vernacular texts silently with full comprehension. The changes made in the script and text format of vernacular texts made reading possible for a wider range of persons than was previously possible. The change from oral to silent reading was virtually completed. No longer did readers read texts out loud with the intention of using them as guides to oratorical performances. Now readers could read and understand ideas, arguments, and scientific observations in the books being produced and disseminated at an increasingly rapid rate.

In certain vernacular *lettre batarde* books, punctuation was borrowed from Latin university books and was calculated to guide the eye of the private reader, rather than to regulate the voice of the professional reader. Aristocratic books of the fifteenth century regularly used paragraph signs, underlining, and capitalization to divide texts into intellectual, rather than rhetorical units. (Saenger, 1997, 270–271)

The changes from common, out-loud reading to private, silent reading of word-separated vernacular script took place in Italy during the first half of the fourteenth century, a full fifty years earlier than in northern Europe. It may not be an overstatement to say that without word-separated script, with all its accompanying graphic aids, the Renaissance—the rebirth of learning in Europe, which began in Italy—and the spread of humanism might not have taken place, or at least might have been delayed for many years. For instance, two books of Dante's *Divine Comedy,* the *Inferno* and *Paradisio,* were composed in Italian and enjoyed a wide readership. Because more and more lay aristocrats and members of the great Italian families desired books written in the vernacular, scribes copied them in a version of the highly readable *cursiva formata,* created in Italy specifically for transcribing lay literature.

Some Italian scribes revered the ancient texts written in unseparated *scriptura continua* and still used this ancient script for "display" books—those to be placed on exhibition—but these scribes were practical enough to realize that the new word-separated script was here to stay. The scribes also imitated those distinctive features of earlier scripts that would make vernacular, word-separated texts still easier to read. For instance, they extended the vertical stroke of the letter "t" above the height of the other letters. They used capital letters for proper names. They marked divided words to be continued on the next line of a manuscript, using not our hyphen but a mark like the acute accent. And they used Arabic numerals—very non-Roman—to foliate the pages. These humanist scribes also employed what we would now recognize as commas, periods, and capital letters. But, we are told, "[the] humanist scribe's most original contribution was the parenthesis, a mark designed to give a graphic representation of the aside, a device of ancient oratorical eloquence. The parenthesis in fifteenth-century humanist texts permitted the private, silent reader to recreate vicariously what in antiquity had been an oral experience" (Saenger, 1997, 272).

The dramatic aside, which moderns may find strange in Shakespearean theatrical soliloquies, was a natural continuation of the time-honored, ancient aside. We still use the upright curved lines of the parenthesis—the singular form referring to either or both of the marks—to show explanatory or qualifying phrases and clauses. The use of dashes to set off written asides has now become common, especially with informal writing, even though traditional writers believe the dash should be used sparingly, for they consider it not acceptable in formal standard prose.

The spread of the new mode of writing—the *lettre hybrida* and the improved humanistic *textualis*— throughout Western Europe in the late fourteenth and fifteen centuries brought about significant changes in the reading habits of the aristocracy and the urban elite. First, authors who once wrote dense and complex theological, scholastic, and scientific books in Latin now wrote books in the vernacular on those topics for educated lay readers. "Just as separated written Latin had facilitated the birth of scholasticism, separated vernacular writing allowed for the transference of the subtleties of full developed scholastic thought to a new lay audience" (Saenger, 1997, 273). Aristocratic laypersons, for example, read arguments on the debate between the philosophical doctrines of nominalism (the idea that concepts, such as truth and virtue, have no reference in reality but exist only as names) and realism (the counterargument that universals are more genuine than so-called real objects in the natural world). These lay readers in the privacy of silent reading could study philosophical debates—just as their scholastic contemporaries did—and make their own decisions as to which positions they accepted as valid.

At the same time, since lay readers could now read silently and in private, they could share unpopular political thoughts. For instance, Charles of France, the brother of Louis XI, left lying around, for any-

one who might just pick it up and read it, a copy of the Roman author Cicero's *De officiis,* with juicy passages underlined advocating the assassination of tyrants. In effect, during the second half of the fourteenth century, the vernacular book became the primary source for ideas urging resistance to oppressive rulers.

And finally, the new private, silent reading had a potent effect upon individuals' religious devotions. As they read vernacular religious books privately, readers were able to work out for themselves their personal relationships to a higher being. Thomas à Kempis, the renowned writer of *The Imitation of Christ* (*De imitatione Christi*), originally written in Latin for his fellow monks, allowed the popular book to be quickly translated into French. The work was soon widely read by members of the Burgundian court in southeastern France.

It is at this time that we first find expressions of the "sacred" nature of the written word, of the idea that readers should read in silence in order to reach the most intense level of spiritual experience. The author Jean Mansel, for instance, in the prologue to his book *Vie de Christ* (*Life of Christ*), "declared that the spoken word is fleeting, while the written word endures, and he called upon knights and princes disposed to devotion for the profit of their souls 'to see' (*voire*) the content of his book" (Saenger, 1997, 275).

Writers of vernacular texts constantly instructed readers to separate themselves from groups in order to read and offer up their individual, silent prayers. Authors of vernacular religious books, of course, used all the graphic aids evolved over the centuries for scholastic Latin texts (punctuation now also included a modification of the medieval *diastole,* a large, comma-shaped mark placed under a line to indicate word separation).

The wave of religious fervor, which spread throughout Europe in the fifteenth century, was made possible largely by religious vernacular books. At the same time, however, silent reading of vernacular religious texts may have added to readers' feelings of spiritual inadequacy, and this in turn might have contributed to religious reform. Changes in word-separated texts had so radically altered reading that lay readers could now hold nonconforming opinions in private and share them with others in writing, which acted as a catalyst to the spread of the Protestant Reformation. The printing press obviously facilitated the spread of radical ideas, but the mode of writing, developed painstakingly by multitudes of uncelebrated scribes and authors over a period of some eight hundred years, was a major factor in the dissemination of new ideas about political and religious freedom, individual study, religious contemplation, and personal expression, which, in turn, all contributed to the modern period of Western civilization:

> The printing press would play an important role in the ultimate triumph of Protestantism, but the formulation of reformist religious and political ideas and the receptivity of Europe's elite to making private judgments on matters of conscience owed much to a long evolution that began in the late seventh century and culminated in the fifteenth century in the manner in which men and women read and wrote. This enhanced privacy represented the consummation of the development of separated writing and constituted a crucial aspect of the modern world. (Saenger, 1997, 276)

And that is how we learned to read.

Summary

1. **Changing How We Learned to Read: Changing How We Think**. The changes in the way texts were written from the late seventh century in Ireland through the fifteenth century in Europe transformed the way we read. But the modifications in writing also altered the ways in which our minds work, the ways by which we process and acquire knowledge. And some authors maintain that such changes in written language actually affected the physical makeup of our brains.

    Of particular importance in page composition were changes in word separation and the

addition of punctuation marks. In addition, the language and style of written language changed from that of formal Latin, conveying meaning by inflections and using long, complicated periodic sentences, to that of the analytic vernacular languages, using the word order characteristic of them; in the process, writing changed from unseparated print to word-separated cursive. We changed from a highly individualistic practice of spelling to a generally agreed upon system of spelling. We changed from writing mostly about well-known ancient works to new books as well on such topics as theology, philosophy, and science. And we changed from writing in Latin to writing in the vernacular languages spoken in Europe.

2. **Changes in How We Learned to Read: By Language, Book Production, and the Opening of Schools.** According to recent scholarship, the late Middle Ages was a remarkable time for change in three major areas. The first change was in language. Ancient Greeks and Romans were able to read unseparated, hand-printed, Latin *scriptura continua,* because it represented the language of those who spoke it. The Latin script of the twelfth century, even though it was easy to read for native speakers of the language, was a second language for many of its readers. The change from Latin to word-separated script in the vernacular was responsible for an enormous increase in the number of people who could read. "In 1500, although it is difficult to measure with quantitative precision, a larger percentage of the general population in England and France were competent to read vernacular texts than had ever been the case in ancient Greece or Rome" (Saenger, 1997, 14).

The second great change affecting reading was how books were produced. In antiquity and in the early Middle Ages, books were not only transcribed by hand but were also put together manually, a lengthy and time-consuming process. Such books were extremely precious but not plentiful. With the onset of word-separated script in Ireland in the seventh century, however, scribes no longer had to copy books from the dictation of a colleague. Scribes now transcribed books privately, following a script visually. Word separation thus changed the reading psychology—the actual mental processes—of the scribes. "When copying a word separated book, a medieval Latin scribe, like a modern typist, could with minimal effort, duplicate a literary text by replicating a linear series of word images and signs of punctuation" (Saenger, 1997, 14). In short, instead of listening to another scribe read the pages of a book and attempting to reproduce in writing the spoken words phonetically, the scribe now could simply copy down "word images"—word-separated word for word-separated word—along with the accompanying signs of punctuation. This was still a slow and difficult task, but it was a great deal easier than any previous method.

This practice of copying books visually rather than by dictation was later standardized through a *pecia* system of producing "perfect" books. After the invention of movable type and the printing press in the mid-1440s, the publication of books increased at a furious pace. As a result, "in 1500 books of legible quality . . . were widely available for moderate prices to a readership extending from London to Warsaw" (Saenger, 1999, 14).

The third major change in reading in the late Middle Ages was the opening of new schools in which reading and writing were taught to an ever-increasing number of people. What teachers taught may sound familiar to us; instruction included "word separation, punctuation, and standardized orthography" (Saenger, 1999, 14). The theory of the "whole word" method of teaching reading, which was first used in

medieval Celtic teaching, was even a matter of debate.

The spread of schools to teach reading and writing did not alter the psychology of reading; rather, it was a factor in spreading literacy. As schools were established, the society of late medieval Europe was transformed, for widespread schooling ensured that people other than those in religious orders, scholastics, royalty, or aristocrats could read.

Rich and poor and men and women deciphered meaning by approximately the same processes. The social context of reading thus became crucial in the early modern period when fluent reading, which had largely been the privilege of a restricted elite in the Middle Ages, was translated into the vernacular and disseminated via printed books to the majority of the inhabitants of western Europe. (Saenger, 1999, 15)

Glossary

analytic language—A language, like English, that uses word order and function words—unlike a heavily inflected language like Latin, that uses word endings—to show meaning.

banderole—A ribbon-shaped figure written in the margin of a book, containing added useful information.

chanson de geste—Any one of some eighty Old French epic poems written from the eleventh through the fourteenth century, celebrating the deeds of historical or legendary heroes, especially the adventures of Charlemagne.

codex (plural codices)—A manuscript volume, first used by the early Christians in the first century A.D. for the Scriptures used in their liturgy. One could write on both sides of the parchment pages of codex but on only one side of a papyrus scroll, and a codex was easier to read and handle than a scroll. By the early second century A.D. all Scripture was copied in codex form.

cursive script—Around the 1400s in Europe, cursive script, with successive lowercase letters joined together, was devised. Such a script—as it is today—is much easier physically to do than is the old practice of printing capitals by hand. In printing, cursive was a style that imitated handwriting.

distinctiones—Latin term for logically dividing chapters and further divisions of chapters into separate parts.

foliation—Numbering consecutively the leaves of a book or manuscript by Arabic numerals, now known as "pagination."

folio—A large sheet of paper folded once in the middle, making two leaves of four pages of a book or manuscript. Also a book or manuscript of the largest common size, usually about 15 inches in height.

gloss—In the Middle ages, a gloss was a brief, explanatory note and sometimes translated foreign terms or unusual technical terms, either in the margins or between the lines of a text. Later, a "glossary" referred to a collection of such notes, either at the end of a chapter or book.

iconography—A set of related pictorial illustrations of a particular subject. Exquisite pictures in medieval manuscripts revealed the lives of well-known persons and activities of the time.

illumination—The art of hand-decorating a text, page, or initial with breathtakingly beautiful, full-colored designs, miniature pictures, or lettering. From the Latin *lumen,* meaning "light."

inflected language—A language, like Latin, that conveys meaning by word endings, unlike an analytic language, like English, which conveys meaning chiefly by word order and function words.

lectio—The Latin term for the practice by ancients of conducting a preliminary examination of a text with unseparated letters forming syllables and syllables forming words that preceded the actual comprehension of a text. Later *lectio* meant "a reading" or "lesson." For Christians, the *lection* was a reading from Scripture that forms part of a church sermon. From this original word, we have "lectern," a reading desk from which scriptural passages are read and "lecture," a formal reading or lesson.

lettre batarde—In the first half of the fifteenth century, this new script appeared almost simultaneously in both Latin and the vernacular, becoming a standard text. *Lettre batarde* was known as the "bastard script" because it had evolved as a combination of an earlier Gothic *textualis,* which was difficult to read, and an existing cursive script, *cursiva formata.* Later scholars called this new script by a more polite name, *hybrida,* the "hybrid" script.

lire au coeur—In the fifteenth century, French aristocrats employed this phrase for reading silently and in private, meaning lit-

erally "to read from the heart," rather than out loud, from the mouth.

narratio—For ancient readers, this term meant "to comprehend a text," from the Latin *narrare, gnarus,* "knowing, to know." Our present meaning of "to narrate" is "to tell a story in speech or in writing."

ocular regression—Literally means "looking backward." Ancient readers, trying to comprehend texts with unseparated words, needed to scan the letters backward—as well as forward—in order to make certain that the words they found did indeed contribute to the overal meaning of a sentence.

orthography—The art or study of correct spelling according to established usage, simply stated as standard, conventional spelling practices. The word is derived from the Greek *ortho,* "straight," and *graphen,* "to write," thus meaning literally "to write straight."

parataxis—Writing together clauses and phrases without coordinating or subordinating conjunctions, for example: "It was hot we felt roasted" or "Since it was unbearably hot we went for a swim."

pecia—Medieval practice in which professional scribes produced "correct" copies of standard texts used throughout a university curriculum. Perhaps the word comes from the Latin *peccare,* "to sin," *pecia,* meaning "without error."

periodic sentence—A favorite sentence construction of the ancients in which the main clause or the verb comes at the end, e.g.,"Because of clear skies and no wind to speak of, we landed our plane safely."

praelectio—For an ancient reader of texts with no spaces between words, the practice of "prereading" out loud, an initial survey of the text before reading the text for real.

quire—A set of twenty-four or sometimes twenty-five leaves of four double sheets of parchment or paper of the same size or stock, folded one within another in a manuscript or book. From the Latin *quaterni,* "set of four."

rubricator—In the eleventh century, scribes and rubricators corrected previously written manuscripts by adding accepted punctuation marks, known as *prosodiae.* The word "rubric," from the Latin *rubrica, ruber,* "red," originally referred to the practice of coloring a title, heading, or even an intitial letter of a book section red. Eventually the word "rubric" became the label for any authoritarian rule written in red.

saccade—In reading, a rapid intermittent eye movement across a page, not at a steady, continuous rate, but in a series of "leaps" or "jumps."

scriptura continua—First employed by the ancient Greeks and later by the Romans, the script consisted of strings of letters written together without word separation or with any punctuation marks. Such a way of writing persisted for centuries because texts were written to be read out loud, frequently to audiences.

in silentio—In the Middle Ages, before persons learned to read silently and in private, this term was used to instruct monks and others how to read texts orally in a low, muffled voice. Also known as *submissa vox,* from Latin, to "lower one's voice" and *suppressa vox,* to "suppress one's voice."

stationer—Medieval publisher and bookseller. The term comes from the Latin *stationarius,* possibly from the Latin *station,* "a place of business, station."

textualis—An ancient script of formal Latin, used almost exclusively for copying manuscripts and books in the form of codices.

vernacular—The native language of a people, as distinguished from a second academic or learned language, which for centuries in Europe was Latin.

CHAPTER FOUR

Two Modes of Knowing

Expository and Literary

Let me begin by setting out my argument as baldly as possible and then go on to examine its basis and its consequences. It is this. There are two irreducible modes of cognitive functioning—or more simply two modes of thought—each meriting the status of a "rational kind." Each provides a way of ordering experience, of constructing reality, and the two (though amenable to complementary use) are irreducible to one another. Each also provides ways of organizing representation in memory and of filtering the perceptual world. Efforts to reduce one mode to the other or to ignore one at the expense of the other inevitably fail to capture the rich ways in which people "know" and describe events around them.

(Bruner, 1985, 97)

The cognitive psychologist Jerome Bruner argues that we have two different ways of using our minds. Each, he maintains, is a distinctly separate method of "ordering experience," of trying to make sense of the terribly complex and confusing world in which we live. Each method helps us to put into some sort of order what we remember, to call up our memories and make sense of them. These mental aids (which are human inventions) act as frames—or filters, to use Bruner's term—that assist us in perceiving and understanding our environment. It is crucial

to note here that Bruner does not use the word "thinking." Rather, he employs the word "perceiving," which carries the meaning of apprehending reality through both our minds and our feelings, for we have evidence that our brains have the capacity to "feel" as well as to "think" (see Blake, 1978, 83–94 and Damasio, 1999).

According to Bruner, the two basic ways our brains work are essentially different from each other. Taken together, the two modes make a whole method of apprehending reality. If we use only one mode to the exclusion of the other—if we perceive primarily by rational means and neglect how we feel and learn through nonrational means—then we do so at our own peril, running the risk of denying ourselves a potentially rich and full life.

Two Modes of Knowing

narrative mode of knowing

Telling stories through fiction, poetry, plays, and through oral transmission by elder family members or case histories by patients of physicians and pychiatrists.

paradigmatic mode of knowing

A type of knowing also called rational, abstract, scientific, and mathematical, which, according to the cognitive psychologist, Jerome Bruner, who coined the term, is irreducibly opposed to narrative knowing.

What are the two ways of dealing with our world? How do we describe them? Bruner calls them the **narrative** and **paradigmatic** modes of thought, generally known as stories and exposition. Others call the two modes literary knowing and rational, logical, or scientific knowing.

Why should we be concerned with the idea of two ways of perceiving reality in a consideration of reading? Because it follows that since narration and exposition are two dissimilar ways of knowing, we need to learn how to read the various texts that represent the two modes. To put it simply, we tell and write stories—and poems—not to provide factual, scientific information but to create, through words, emotional experiences. (We do learn from literary texts, of course, but not in the way we learn from informational writing.) And conversely, we read exposition expressly by not allowing our feelings to intrude, but rather to process information as clearly and dispassionately as possible.

Is the contention that there are two inherent modes of knowing valid? Is Bruner correct in stating that these ways of knowing are not only a part of our culture, but are inherently irreducible? There is considerable agreement among scholars not only that these two modes are still alive but that the rational, scientific, paradigmatic mode is ascendant in our culture.

For example, Elliot Eisner, an art educator, broadens the idea of literary knowing beyond literature to include other arts and calls all these activities "aesthetic" modes of knowing:

> The phrase "aesthetic modes of knowing" presents something of a contradiction in our culture. We do not typically associate the aesthetic with knowing. The arts, with which aesthetic is most closely associated, is a matter of the heart. Science is thought to provide the most direct route to knowledge. Hence, "aesthetic modes of knowing" is a phrase that contradicts the conception of knowledge that is most widely accepted. (Eisner, 1985, 23–24)

Not only do we encounter aesthetic modes of knowing through the arts, including literature, but many scientists frequently use aesthetic modes of knowing in their pursuit of scientific knowledge. Eisner cites the scientist Alfred North Whitehead in this regard: "Scientists, Whitehead believes, are drawn to their work not by epistemological motives but by aesthetic ones. The joy of inquiry is the driving motive for their work. Scientists, like artists, formulate new and puzzling questions in order to enjoy the experience of creating answers to them" (1985, 27).

We acquire knowledge through the aesthetic mode of knowing in two ways: First, we come to understand the world through the structures or forms that we create through the aesthetic modes of knowing. Homer created the form of the oral folk epics the *Iliad* and the *Odyssey* to present the elements of a Greek warrior to its people. Likewise, the Irish writer James Joyce created the revolutionary form of the "stream of consciousness" in such novels as *A Portrait of the Artist as a Young Man* and *Ulysses* to reveal the Irish culture to his people. A second kind of knowing derived from the aesthetic mode is the pleasure one enjoys by surrendering to an emotional experience triggered by a piece of art.

The most provocative argument for the value of the aesthetic mode is the claim that through this mode we *create* knowledge. The general opinion toward the scientific mode is that in this way, by contrast, we *find* or *discover* knowledge. The scientist finds the knowledge that the earth is round and that it revolves around the sun. Sophocles in *Oedipus Rex* and Shakespeare in *Hamlet,* on the other hand, create knowledge that parricide, the killing one's father, is a universal taboo.

If we confuse the aesthetic with the scientific mode, the aesthetic is diminished by our cherished belief that we search for knowledge rather than create it. Knowledge, according to this viewpoint, is out there waiting to be found, and the most useful tool for finding it is the scientific method. "If there were greater appreciation for the extent to which knowledge is constructed—something made—there might be a greater likelihood that its aesthetic dimensions would be appreciated" (Eisner, 1985, 32).

Eisner believes that artists—broadly conceived to include musical composers, painters, and architects, as well as writers and occasionally scientists—are capable of using the aesthetic mode. If so, we would prefer to think of the aesthetic mode of knowing as best viewed along a continuum, with the purest form of aesthetic knowing at one end and the least aesthetic, the most scientific, at the opposite end.

For Bruner, the two modes of knowing cannot be placed on a continuum; rather, they are irreducible. Our concern here is to ask if there are indeed two different modes of knowing, what the characteristics are of each, and more crucially, how do we make sense of them?

Bruner argues that the paradigmatic, the most fully developed in our culture, fulfills the idea of a formal system of observation, description, and explanation and is based upon the rational functions of categorization and conceptualization. Because the paradigmatic mode has been developed over the millennia in Western culture, we know a great deal more about it than we do about the aesthetic. We have produced powerful systems—mental "prosthetic" devices, he calls them, analogous to artificial limbs—for carrying on paradigmatic thought, such as human inventions of logic, mathematics, and the algorithms used in the hard sciences (e.g., physics, chemistry, and astronomy) to conduct their research. Paradigmatic knowing leads to good theory, tight analysis, logical proof, and empirical discovery guided by reasoned hypotheses. It follows that this kind of knowing requires a special kind of reading.

The narrative mode, on the other hand, leads to rousing stories, elegant poems, gripping drama, believable historical accounts, and even perceptive case histories for physicians and psychiatrists (see Coles, 1998). Seldom do we find in hard science narrative or poetry, and if we do apply scientific techniques such as New Criticism to narrative, "we replace the narrative by a paradigmatic structure" (Bruner, 1985, 99). Any detached, purely analytic, rational analysis of a story, poem, novel, or play then exhibits paradigmatic thought rather than narrative perception. Not only do we read a literary text in a different way from the way we read a scientific text, but we also need a different language to discuss either mode of knowing. The literary critic Caroline F.E. Spurgeon, for example, once did a paradigmatic analysis of dominant images in Shakespearean plays "to throw new light on the poet and his work" (Spurgeon, 1952, ix). In the play *Hamlet,* she found a great many "images of sickness, disease or blemish of the body . . . and we discover that the idea of an ulcer or tumour, as descriptive of the unwholesome condition of Denmark morally, is, on the whole, the dominant one" (Spurgeon, 1935, 316). We can, however, also discover such a conclusion by an intuitive, literary response.

Bruner finds it unfortunate that the psychology of thought has concentrated on the paradigmatic mode to the virtual exclusion of the narrative mode. At the same time for Bruner, philosophy, the parent of psychology, has been concerned only with study-

ing how paradigmatic knowing works, how mind comes to know the world, to represent it, to reach right conclusions about it, to avoid errors, and to achieve generality and abstraction (Bruner, 1985, 102). The reason for this state of affairs is that scholars in psychology and philosophy desire their disciplines to be more like the hard natural sciences, more rigorous and scientific, than are the social sciences. As evidence, Bruner offers this example:

> Piaget, for all his genius, saw the growth of mind as paralleling the growth of science—or vice versa. There is no reasoned way in his system of characterizing the difference between the prattling of the department gossip and a Homer, a Joyce, or a Hardy. For some reason, the nature and growth of thought that are necessary for the elaboration of great stories, great histories, great myths—have not seemed very attractive or challenging to most of us [cognitive psychologists]. So we have left the job to the literary scholars and linguists, to the folklorists and anthropologists. And they have studied not the process, but the product, the tales rather than the tellers. (Bruner, 1985, 103)

In short, Bruner believes that the "outcomes produced by the two modes of thought could neither contradict nor corroborate the other," calling this "a very radical claim" (Bruner, 1985, 112, 113).

But such a claim is not really so radical. Most of us unconsciously accept that there are two mutually exclusive modes of knowing or that many times we confuse the two modes, and thus we may try to retrieve facts from a poem or attempt to prove a piece of empirical evidence by a feeling or opinion. The reality of a story cannot be proved true or false by empirical evidence. At the same time, we verify paradigmatic thought not by opinion or by feeling but by logic, rational thought, objective observation, and by the accumulation of empirical data. "Each [narrative and paradigmatic thought] is a version of the world, and to ask which depicts the real world is to ask a question that even modern metaphysicians believe to be undecidable" (Bruner, 1985, 113).

Theory of Multiple Intelligences

Theory proposed by Howard Gardner in his 1985 book, *Frames of Mind: The Theory of Multiple Intelligences*, which are the following: linguistic, musical, logico-mathematical, spatial, bodily kinesthetic, and personal intelligences, consisting of the intrapersonal and interpersonal intelligences. For Gardner, the personal intelligences overarch all the others.

Howard Gardner, another respected cognitive psychologist, addresses the problem and identifies seven discrete ways of knowing in his *Frames of Mind: The Theory of Multiple Intelligences* (1985): linguistic, musical, logico-mathematical, spatial, bodily-kinesthetic, and the personal intelligences, which he divides into the interpersonal and intrapersonal. In a later book, *Intelligence Reframed: Multiple Intelligences for the 21st Century,* he considers "several new candidate intelligences, including 'naturalist,' 'spiritual,' 'existential,' and 'moral' intelligences" (Gardner, 1999, 4).

How do people best learn the personal intelligences (which we maintain are directly related to literary knowing)? As Gardner explains, we acquire them through core myths, rituals, and commonly shared stories. As we experience familiar tales, we learn and eventually internalize crucial intrapersonal and extrapersonal knowledge and skills. Like Bruner, Gardner points out that the presently dominant way of knowing—that is, what is generally perceived to be "intelligence" in our schools and in society at large—is the logical-mathematical intelligence. This view exists to a large degree because of the writings like those of the developmental psychologist Jean Piaget. Gardner acknowledges the power of Piaget's view of knowing—together with his theory of intellectual development—but he believes it represents the narrow position of the laboratory scientist, a "brilliant portrait of that form of intellectual growth which is valued most highly in Western scientific and philosophical traditions" (Gardner, 1985, 20).

Gardner also has problems with Piaget's theoretical model of knowing. He sees Piaget's theory as only one kind of mental development, and one that is less important to people in non-Western cultures and, as we have learned, for nonliterate people—and which may only be applicable to a minority of individuals, even in the West. In addition, Piaget's model ignores the steps in developing mental competence in occupations or professions other than those of laboratory

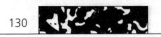

scientists and similar workers; the mental development of artists, writers, dramatists, musicians, lawyers,
athletes, and political statesmen are not addressed.
The tasks created by Piaget are all drawn from the laboratory benches and blackboards of the biologist. In
a way, virtually the only model of intellectual progress
taught directly in our schools, which thus becomes
a part of our cultural inheritance, is Piaget's theory
of scientific knowing.

If Gardner is correct, what does he say about other
intelligences? And of what relevance is his theory of
multiple intelligences to our concern with literary
knowing? The core capacity of an intrapersonal
intelligence is an understanding of our own feelings,
an access to the full range of our emotional person.
If we have a sophisticated intrapersonal intelligence,
we discriminate among our feelings, name them, and
comprehend how they work in all aspects of our lives.
At the simplest level, we use our intrapersonal intelligence to tell the difference between elementary
pleasure and pain. At the highest level, though,
intrapersonal knowing allows us to note and translate into language our own highly complicated and
subtle feelings. Examples of persons with supremely
honed intrapersonal intelligences are fiction writers,
dramatists, poets, psychiatrists, and therapists.

The core capacity of interpersonal intelligence,
which turns us from within ourselves outward
towards others, is the ability to note and make distinctions between feelings in other individuals—in
particular, their moods, temperaments, motivations,
and intentions. When we are children, our interpersonal intelligence allows us to distinguish among people around us and to become aware of their various
states of mind. At an advanced stage, our mature grasp
of interpersonal intelligence permits us to read the
intentions and desires of the people we come in
contact with—even when their purposes are not
explicitly stated and may even be hidden to themselves—and enables us to act upon this information. What kind of people are known for their
superior grasp of interpersonal intelligence, for

understanding the behavior of many people and of having the talent to influence those people to behave in certain ways? They come from all walks of life but can be political and religious leaders, such as Mahatma Gandhi, Abraham Lincoln, Eleanor Roosevelt, and Martin Luther King, Jr., as well as lesser-known persons such as teachers, ministers, priests, therapists, counselors, and wise elders.

This fully developed sense of self is the highest achievement of human beings and is the "crowning capacity which supersedes and presides over more mundane and partial forms of intelligence" (Gardner, 1985, 242). The essence of these intelligences is the skill to use symbols, and without a sophisticated grasp of language and literary knowing, broadly conceived, we are able to cope with only the most elementary and unorganized judgment among feelings. Armed, however, with a refined command of the personal intelligences, we have the potential to make sense of the full range of human experience from all the people we encounter. In summary, "The less a person understands his own feelings, the more he will fall prey to them. The less a person understands the feelings, the responses, and the behavior of others, the more likely he will interact inappropriately with them and therefore fail to secure his proper place within the larger community" (Gardner, 1985, 254).

frozen language

Precious literature of a culture the people will not let die, such as Cervantes' *Don Quixote*, Shakespeare's plays, and Lincoln's "Second Inaugural Address," which is literally carved in stone. Term coined by Martin Joos in his little book, *The Five Clocks*.

The personal intelligences are crucial to our very existence, but how do we learn them? We do not learn them through scientific, logico-mathematical knowing, which deals primarily with the human inventions of logic, mathematics, systematic and objective observation, and abstract theory. We acquire a sophisticated personal intelligence by mastering symbol systems, myths, legends—the common core literature of a culture. Generally speaking, we reach this goal by mastering literary knowing. (The linguist Martin Joos calls this precious literature of a culture, the texts we will not let die, **frozen language**. Such texts as Lincoln's Gettysburg Address and Second Inaugural Address, which are so revered they are

inscribed on marble, are examples of frozen language (Joos, 1967).

But simply reading or seeing worthwhile literature by ourselves is not enough to teach us the personal intelligences. We need to recognize that experiencing literature is—as it was for the ancient Greeks—a social activity. We need to read and see literature—including concerts, movies, TV shows, and plays—but it is essential that we allow ourselves to enter into these works together, to respond orally and in writing to what we have experienced, and to discuss out responses with others. Only through this process can we learn about ourselves, about how we feel and think and learn about others. These are the social and cultural knowledge and social skills that worthwhile literature can impart. In essence, "through formal tutoring, or through literature, rituals, and other symbolic forms, the culture helps the growing individual to make discriminations about his feelings, or about the other persons in his milieu" (Gardner, 1985, 251).

The personal intelligences overarch all other intelligences. "Perhaps," Gardner hypothesizes, "it makes more sense to think of knowledge of self and others at a higher level [than that of the other intelligences], a more integrated form of intelligence at the behest of the culture and of historical factors, one more truly emergent, one that ultimately comes to control and to regulate more 'primary orders' of intelligence" (Gardner, 1985, 274).

The following chart presents, in an admittedly oversimplified way, the striking differences between the two ways of knowing. It is well known that such outlines reduce extremely intricate situations into less complex terms, but the description will at least provide food for thought and a basis for discussion. Unlike Bruner, we are not certain that the two modes are irreducible. Rather, we believe we can better understand their characteristics by thinking of them as occurring along a continuum. Viewing the features of these two ways of knowing as being opposites, we come to think of them as antithetical,

as one mode as versus the other. But we know from reading many kinds of texts that writers often use language representing both kinds of knowing within the same text. The historian Shelby Foote, for instance, uses the techniques of fiction in his acclaimed and immensely popular three-volume history, *The Civil War,* and he aptly identifies the way of knowing it represents by the book's subtitle: *A Narrative.* On the other hand, the philosopher Plato, explaining the ultimate of abstract ideas—that of the nature of reality— uses the poetic device of metaphor in his famous description of "The Cave."

Logic-Mathematical, Scientific Knowing and Literary Knowing

Scientific Knowing	Literary Knowing
Deals with abstractions and generalizations, especially in pure mathematics. Considered by most people to be the highest form of knowing.	Deals with reality though the concrete and specific, such as objects, events creatures, and human beings.
Seeks to discover absolute truths, ideal, never-changing realities such as gravity, the Pythagorean theorem, and relativity.	Teaches us to tolerate ambiguities and to accept irony and paradox in our lives.
Perceives reality by disinterested, objective observation, and logical, rational methods such as equations, propositions, rules, and laws.	Approaches reality through stories, poems, songs, and plays about people.
Generally ignores what cannot be explained by a logical system of reasoning and believes that if something cannot be observed and measured, it does not exist.	Concedes that there are forces in life not perceived by rational means alone. Hamlet's observation seems apt here: "There's more than is dreamt of in your philosophy, Horatio."
Insists on objective detachment on the grounds that emotions distort observations and and judgments.	Requires involvement and participation within a human and ever-widening community.

Usually amoral and does not admit the ethical concerns of good and evil.	Constantly deals with the notions of good and evil, right and wrong. Melville's *Billy Budd*, Hawthorne's *The Scarlet Letter*, Twain's *Huckleberry Finn*, Morrison's *Beloved*, and Sophocles' *Antigone* spring to mind as outstanding examples of works with this focus.
Ignores a divine being as an explanation of reality.	Insists on the preciousness of the of the individual as the spiritual sings it, "His eye is on the sparrow." Frequently is concerned with universal matters, such as the existence of a divine being, tending to believe with Hamlet that "there's a divinity that shapes our ends, rough-hew them how we will."

Expository Texts

What are the characteristics of expository texts? Here we turn to an example of a particular kind of expository writing, that of an encyclopedia entry, which we anticipate will be detached, objective, and informative.

Observe carefully the kinds of direct sentences and notice in particular that the author writes not of an individual tiger but of the general behavior of all tigers, employing the words "the tiger" and "tigers." The text is a model of inductive thinking, a form of logical reasoning in which we draw conclusions about members of a group after observing a number of the members of that class. Although we accept this kind of writing unconsciously, assuming it has always been with us, it is a fairly recent invention, perhaps some five hundred years old.

ENTRY FROM *THE WORLD BOOK ENCYCLOPEDIA*

Tiger is the largest member of the cat family. People admire the tiger for its strength and beauty, but they also fear it because it has been known to kill and occasionally eat people. Yet wild tigers prefer to avoid human beings. Tigers that kill and eat people are most often sick or wounded animals that can no longer hunt their natural prey. A hungry tiger may also attack people if prey is extremely scarce. Wild tigers are found only in Asia. Until the 1800's, many tigers lived throughout much of the southern half of the continent. Now only a few wild tigers remain in most countries, and none of the animals are left in Iran and Pakistan.

The life of a tiger. Adult tigers usually live alone though they are not unfriendly with one another. Two tigers may meet on their nightly rounds, rub heads in a typical cat greeting, and then part. Several tigers may share in eating a killed prey. Adult males often claim their own territory and try to keep other males out. In areas with abundant prey, such territories may average about 20 square miles (52 square kilometers). The male tiger marks trees in his territory with his scent and urine. The scent tells other tigers that the territory is occupied. A male's territory overlaps the territories of two of more females. Female territories are smaller than a male's. Although each tiger wanders alone, they communicate with each other. In addition to scent, they communicate with sounds, including a roar that can be heard for up to 2 miles (3.2 kilometers) or more. Some tigers do not have territories and travel widely.

Scientific classification. Tigers belong to the genus *Panthera* in the cat family, *Felidae*. All tigers are of the same species, *P. tigris*. (Schaller, 1998, 283–285)

This selection, from *The World Book Encyclopedia,* is a fine example of exposition, writing aimed at presenting ordered information that is a consequence of systematic observation and disciplined thought, the result of what we call the scientific method. The writing is arranged in a clearly logical structure and is presented in a straightforward manner. There are, for instance, no examples of figurative language such as similes and metaphors. It presents unambiguous information by way of a technical vocabulary, not an emotional experience open to varied interpretations.

In addition to the information cited above, the entry also deals with these additional topics: the body of the tiger, tigers and people, and how the tiger hunts. The author makes general statements about tigers based on data collected from observation—a great deal firsthand—of many individual tigers. (It is important to note that the author is a world-renowned naturalist, who, we expect, would write an exemplary expository piece.)

The second example of expository writing—although it demonstrates strikingly precise observation—is less objective than the first selection. The author, another acclaimed naturalist, Peter Matthiessen, adds to his exposition emotionally laden words and gives voice to his own personal opinions and feelings.

In this selection, Matthiessen reports on his firsthand observation of the evidence that he is in the ominous territory of a tiger—its "last redoubt"—whose familiar name is the Amur tiger. This legendary beast, also called the Siberian tiger, is encountered, as we have learned, in the wild only in the sparsely populated Russian Far East. If we were to meet this great cat, we would be obliged to address it by its formal Latin name, *Panther tigris altaica.*

The "Arseniev" the author refers to is Vladimir K. Arseniev, a young Russian army lieutenant, geographer, and naturalist, who by horseback made three expeditions between 1902 and 1905 to map the wild Primorsk Krai, or Maritime Province, of Siberia.

How might we read this piece of expository writing? First, we go over it rather quickly for a general impression. After we have done this, we consider these questions: How do we feel about the piece? What is our general emotional response? What are the one or two things that stand out in our minds about tigers?

At any rate, awareness that a tiger is close by lends a certain edge to walking in the taiga. Scrapes were numerous among the ferns of the forest floor, and a fine big print in the dried mud sprang at the eye. ("The perfectly distinct and fresh impressions of an immense cat's paw, standing out sharply printed in the muddy track," as Arseniev describes it. The water had not yet found its way into this quite-fresh pugmark.) High up on a tree trunk, deep scratches marked the place where a tiger on hind legs had sharpened its two-inch claws by raking them downward with the powerful foreshoulders that, together with the stabbing action of its canine teeth and its bone-shearing incisors, allow it to overpower much larger prey. A urine scent post on a hard-rubbed elm was another signal to other tigers that this was an established territory. Knowing that such a powerful creature had paused right here in these silent trees, the fire-striped coat rising and falling as it breathed and listened, was exhilarating, to say the least. Besides excellent hearing, tigers have binocular and color vision. In combination with tail lashing, which raises the black tail tuft in warning, a threatened tiger may rotate its ears to show the bold black-ringed spots on the backs; otherwise their markings have evolved as camouflage adaptations for tall grass, reeds, and woodlands, just as the spots of leopard and jaguar reflect the dappled lights of wind-danced leaves. (Matthiessen, 2000, 27)

Now I read it over a second time for a deeper and richer appreciation. I know from the first sentence that this will be more personal than the encyclopedia entry. The writer tells me that an "awareness" of a tiger close by "lends a certain edge" to walking in the taiga. Rather than "knowing" or being "conscious" of a tiger, the writer is "aware," a very old word, suggesting "watchfulness" or "being vigilant."

The writer alternates observation with his prior knowledge of tigers. He notes the tiger's footprints (pugmarks), deep scratches made on a tree trunk to sharpen its claws, and a scent post where the tiger urinates to mark his territory. And Matthiessen reveals his excitement—very unscientific-like—by tell us that the experience is "exhilarating." He continues to educate us about the tiger: its hearing, color vision, tail lashing, ear rotation, and coat markings as having evolved for the purpose of camouflage. He

ends the informative paragraph, however, with a most poetic phrase, "the dappled lights of wind-danced leaves." This final phrase produces an image of exciting beauty, the experience heightened by the presence of an unbelievably powerful, beautiful, and alien creature.

What do we make of these two pieces of writing? Why do we label them both as expository, and in this case, characteristically scientific? We do so mainly because the intent of the writers is to report on observations of the natural world. Even though one excerpt is detached and impersonal while the other reveals the author's personal opinions and feelings, both are primarily informative. How do we resolve our puzzlement about categorizing both pieces? If we think of the two selections along a continuum, we have no trouble with identifying one as more expository than the other.

Reading Expository (Informational) Texts

Now that we have examined two exemplary models of expository texts by acknowledged masters of nature writing, what conclusions may we draw from them?

Reading Informational Texts

Purpose. The primary purpose of informational texts is to impart knowledge, derived from observation and experience.

Major Informational Text Structures. The major categories of informational writing are as follow:
- describing
- defining
- classifying
- comparing and contrasting
- arguing (persuading)

Critical Thinking Strategies for Reading Informational Texts. The major categories of critical thinking strategies are as follow:

- accepting informational text structures
- initially surveying the text for the "big picture"
- determining the writer's stance
- deciding on the main focus of the text
- picking out major ideas
- comprehending meanings of specialized words
- drawing conclusions
- evaluating what has been read, according to criteria

Practical Strategies for Reading Informational Texts. The major categories of practical strategies are as follow:

- initial quick reading for a major impression
- subsequent close reading for substantiating the first impression
- annotating the text (making personal marks on the text, e.g., underlinings, encircling, drawing arrows, and so forth)
- jotting down words, phrases, questions (questioning comprehension of meaning)
- looking up words in a dictionary for precise meaning
- making an informal outline to find structure
- recognizing the author's intent
- paraphrasing or summarizing the text
- testing the validity of the text
- considering emotionally laden words and
- finally verifying the main idea of the text

Literary (Narrative and Poetic) Texts

From our careful attention to the two preceding expository texts, we have found the task of describing this mode of knowing not as simple as we might have first assumed. In any event, we can state with some confidence that expository texts generally share many of the same features.

We now turn to another kind of text, literary writing, to describe its salient characteristics. One problem here is that we have less agreement about how to read literary texts than we do about compre-

hending expository texts. This may be because over the centuries we have developed a number of powerful mental aids, such as abstract thought, logical analysis, experimental methods, and techniques for observing and writing exposition.

In order to differentiate between expository and literary knowing, we move to an iconic example of a literary text on the same topic as the preceding examples of exposition, a poem, "The Tiger," by the printer, illustrator, poet, and mystic, William Blake (1757–1827).

How might we read this piece of literary writing? As we did for the expository text, we read it the first time right through—preferably out loud—our chief purpose being to find the emotions triggered by it. What has the poem done to us? How do we feel after having read it? After we have acknowledged our feelings, we ask ourselves questions like these: What's it all about? What's going on here? What does it all add up to?

THE TIGER

William Blake

Tiger! Tiger! burning bright
In the forests of the night,
What immortal hand or eye
Could frame thy fearful symmetry?

In what distant deeps or skies
Burnt the fire of thine eyes?
On what wings dare he aspire?
What the hands dare seize the fire?

And what shoulder, and what art,
Could twist the sinews of thy heart?
And when thy heart began to beat,
What dread hand? And what dread feet?

What the hammer? And what the chain?
In what furnace was thy brain?
What the anvil? What dread grasp
Dare its deadly terrors clasp?

When the stars threw down their spears,
And watered heaven with their tears,

Did he smile his work to see?
Did he who made the Lamb make thee?

Tiger! Tiger! burning bright
In the forests of the night,
What immortal hand or eye
Dare frame thy fearful symmetry?

In a startling fashion, the poet is speaking directly to a mysterious and powerful creature, the tiger. With a series of direct, intimate questions, he demands of the tiger Who could have created you? How could he have accomplished such an amazing feat? And incredibly, how could your creator have brought into being such creatures as you and the Lamb? The poet is asking a basic question about the nature of the ultimate being. (The same question is posed by Hamlet in his third soliloquy: "To be or not to be. That is the question.")

Now we read over the poem a second time, stanza by stanza, even word by word, known by its French term as ***explication de texte***, or close reading, to allow the images and associations triggered by the words to form in our minds. We may find the poem so hard to penetrate, though, that it is almost impossible to recount the complete train of images, emotions, and thoughts aroused by it.

Immediately with the first words "Tiger! Tiger!" we are startled by the exclamations! The poet is shouting at the legendary beast! (But can we imagine ourselves talking politely to a caged tiger in a zoo: "Mr. Tiger, how are you today?") Can we see ourselves as the poet does—of meeting this great stalking cat in the wild and shouting at it: "Tiger! Tiger! Who created you!" or "Tiger! Who on the earth and in the heavens could have made you?"

Throughout the poem, the questions to the tiger follow one after the other: What immortal hand or eye could frame your fearful symmetry? In what sea or sky were your fiery eyes made? Who twisted the sinews of your heart and caused it to beat? In what furnace and on what anvil was your brain hammered out? (We take the puzzling lines "when the stars threw down their tears/ And watered heaven

explication de texte

The French term for what is known in English as "close reading." A method of literary criticism in which the interrelated details of a written work are examined and analyzed in an effort to understand its structure and discover an inherent meaning.

with their tears" to refer to the creation of the universe.) And finally, the poet asks: "If this omnipotent force created you, Tiger, how could it at the same time have created the Lamb?"

Finally, we return to the repeated final stanza, which is identical to the opening stanza, except with one arresting exception, the substitution of the word "dare" for the original "could." After the explosive exclamations of the first stanzas and the percussive questions in the following stanzas, we re-read the concluding stanza in a hushed, reverent voice.

As we look back at the poem still another time, we begin to unravel some of the overwhelming complexity of this literary text by attending to some of its poetic features: images, words, ambiguous phrases, figurative language, repetitions, and structures. We need to stress that the elements overlap, that images are produced by words and unusual juxtapositions of words and that figurative language produces ambiguous language.

Here are just a few of the poem's images: "Tiger! Tiger! burning bright," "in the forests of the night," "twist the sinews," "in what furnace," and "stars threw down their spears."

And we note some of the vivid words and phrases such as these: "frightful symmetry" and "the fires of thine eyes."

As we look closely, we see how the poet has made use of figurative language. We find many examples of his employing words for parts of something to represent a whole from which the part is taken, as in "What the hands dare seize the fire?" the figure of speech we call synecdoche. Other examples of this ancient poetic device include "What shoulders . . . could twist the sinews of thy heart?" and "What dread hand and what dread feet?"

As we read over the poem, we pick out repeated words and phrases, and see a pattern of related words emerging, which point to a governing motif. For instance, we observe repetitions of words related to "flame," such as "burning" and "fire," connoting heat and brilliance. In addition, we see the words "dread" and "dare" repeated most significantly.

Finally, we draw back from single words and phases to make out several designs. First is the overall design, that of the poet asking a number of surprising questions of a great, wild beast. Then there are a number of other structures, such as the distinctive poetic feet of the lines (accented and unaccented syllables), rhythm, and rhyme schemes—both end rhyme and the ancient initial rhyme, also called alliteration.

Although most contemporary poets no longer use regular verse patterns, this poem is made up of five stanzas of generally four-beat (tetrameter) couplets. The couplets consist mostly of end–rhyming words, except for "eye/symmetry." Furthermore, Blake uses the oldest of English rhymes, initial rhyme, in which the beginning sound of two or three of the words in a line are identical: "burning bright," "frame the fearful," and "distant days."

The total effect is that of a somber, serious, perfectly designed structure of words, images, and sounds, all parts fitting inextricably together in an organic whole. The tightly controlled couplets, the regular rhythm and rhymes all contribute to a perfectly designed edifice dedicated to addressing several of the most basic human questions: Who made all living creatures? What is the nature of being? How could a higher being create such startlingly different creatures as the Tiger and the Lamb (as well as me)?

Old Criticism

A theory of literary criticism in which the the chief emphasis is on the author's purpose in writing the work, an interest in the mind and personality of the poet, writer of fiction, or playwright.

New Criticism

A theory of literary criticism with the the chief emphasis on the text, designed to discover the intrinsic meaning of the literary work. The approach focuses on the close examination (close reading) of a text with minimum regard for the biographical or historical circumstances in which it was produced.

Reading Literary (Poetic and Narrative) Texts

Attitudes toward reading literary texts have evolved over the last century through the following stages: (1) emphasis on the writer and his aims—"authorial intent"—known as the **Old Criticism**; (2) emphasis on the text, developed into a school of literary interpretation by critics and writers—known as **New Criticism**—whose purpose was to discover through carefully prescribed moves the intrinsic meaning of a literary text; and (3) emphasis on the reader and his or her individual, idiosyncratic recon-

Reader Response

A theory of literary criticism in which the the chief emphasis is on the reader's personal interpretation of a text. The theory is concerned with the relationship between the text and reader and reader and text, with the stress on the different ways by which a reader participates in reading a text.

struction of the meaning of a text, known as **Reader Response**.

The approach of New Criticism to reading a literary text with an accepted meaning by a specially trained, privileged few, which evolved into an approach that insists rather that every reader is obligated to reconstruct his or her own meanings resulted in a democritization of reading literary texts. The application of Reader Response theory, with its assumptions and methods, to classroom activities is known as Classroom Reader Response. Here are the basic assumptions forming the foundation of the recently developed stance toward reading literary texts.

Assumptions Underlying Classroom Reader Response

1   *Primary emphasis is on the reader's response to a text.* With this method, the emphasis is not solely on one's examination of a text as a text but, rather, is principally on the reader's response to the text. The work itself, of course, is not insignificant, for we all know that Mark Twain's *Huckleberry Finn* is quite different from the yellow pages of a telephone book. The practical result of this assumption, though, is that each reader is recognized as existing uniquely—as a result of many factors, such as age, gender, education, experiences, culture, race, and so forth—and that the reader's response will be a direct result of a mysterious combination of these factors.

2   *Reader creates personal meaning.* Rather than finding someone else's meaning—whether it is the teacher's or that of the teacher's previous professors or the meaning declared over years and formalized within some canon—the reader creates his or her own meaning of the text. The implication of this assumption is that the reader is literally creative, and as a result, with confidence, eventually becomes a "courageous" reader, trusting himself or herself to create rich, satisfying responses to literature.

3   *Feelings are allowed.* Since readers' initial responses to worthwhile pieces of literature are emotional, readers are "allowed," even encouraged, to respond emotionally. With Classroom Reader Response, feelings are okay. Related to this notion, readers accept feelings aroused by a piece because it is through emotions that readers enter into a work.

4   *Memories and associations are encouraged.* When readers permit memories evoked by a literary piece to arise from their unconscious, and when they accept associations related to these experiences—and to other works of literature and even to movies, television shows, and popular songs—they are able to relate literature to their own lives in a powerfully significant way. Those who read a literary text from a traditional stance, our experience has shown, seldom see a poem or story as being relevant to their lives. This is not a trivial point. Literature is a special way of knowing only if one accepts the fact that it is, and only if the reader lets the piece release deep personal memories and associations. We have found that allowing memories to surface through and from a reading and by making available one's response to trusted readers is the single most potent way for readers to perceive literature as a special way of knowing.

5   *Intuition is invoked.* After readers have allowed themselves to become emotionally involved in a piece, and have let themselves experience the piece through memories and associations, they learn to trust themselves to give an immediate, intuitive reaction to the piece. Authors have found that when we ask readers of any age to take a few minutes to relate or write out immediate responses, that primary reaction is invariably the one they stick to. What remains for the readers is to find out why they responded in the way they did and to justify their responses to themselves.

6 *Close reading techniques are used to substantiate initial responses.* Only after readers have gained enough self-confidence to give beginning responses do they then move to close reading techniques in order to justify their original responses. With objective criticism, readers traditionally make an educated guess at the correct interpretation of a text only after having collected evidence by systematic, step-by-step gathering of details. In the Classroom Reader Response approach, though, readers use close reading techniques to discover why they responded the way they did.

7 *Readers share responses with others in a learning community.* The assumption that reading and responding to literature is essentially a social event that occurs within a learning community is the bedrock upon which Classroom Reader Response rests. When readers share their literary responses with others (especially with fellow readers under the guidance of trained and sensitive teachers), their responses are validated. Such common experiences often offer varying viewpoints that contribute to deepening and widening responses, while, at the same time, sharing responses helps to correct surface-level misreadings.

On a higher level, though, sharing responses within a learning community is a natural way for readers to become acculturated, to participate in the ways of living accepted by a culture. Since worthwhile literary works imply personal and social codes of behavior, reading and responding to literature within a learning community make the members aware of the mostly unwritten codes of personal, social, and moral behavior endorsed by a culture.

8 *Readers come to understand responses as reflections of their distinct personalities.* As readers become increasingly sophisticated in Classroom Reading Response, they are able to understand how their particular responses reflect their unique

personalities. Here are some of the general characteristics of literary texts, broadly applied to poetry and narrative.

Reading Literary Texts

Purposes. The primary purposes are to trigger emotional experiences and provide—mostly indirectly—lessons for living.

Major Literary Text Structures. The major categories are poetry and narrative, with many subgenres.

Major Strategies of Classroom Reader Response.
- initial personal, emotional response
- feeling response
- memory response
- close reading after initial response
- choosing available stances to broaden and deepen personal responses (psychological, gender, mythic, moral, and personal)

Practical Strategies for Reading Narration
- initial reading for feeling and overall meaning
- annotating texts with personal marks
- responding to major questions—What happens? (Plot) Who are the people? What are they like? How do they change? (Character) Where does the story take place? How does the setting affect the meaning? (Setting) Choosing evidence from the text to support your meaning (Close reading)
- discussing with others your meaning
- comprehending why you responded the way you did

Practical Strategies for Reading Poetry.
- accepting a poem as a poem
- reading the poem aloud
- responding first emotionally—How do I feel after this poetic experience?
- rereading the poem closely and responding to questions like these—How do I feel about this

poem? What does it mean to me? How do I picture the images? How does figurative language
work (simile, metaphor, synecdoche, metonymy,
and so forth)?

- what effects do structures, rhythm, rhyme, and
sounds have upon the overall meaning? How do
all the aspects of the poem contribute to its
organic whole?
- discussing what your have learned about your-
self and others from the poem (metacognition)
- discovering why you responded the way you
did (hypermetacognition)

Summary

1 **Two Ways of Knowing: Expository and
Literary**. There are two ways of knowing—two
modes of cognition—and thus two ways of writing and reading. One is known by many names:
For the Greek philosopher Plato, it was abstract
thinking. We have variously called it logico-
mathematical, rational, scientific, expository,
and informational. The other kind of knowing
is generally called literary knowing, which
includes poetry, drama, and narrative, and it is
far older and was at one time the sole mode of
knowing. The archetypal examples of literary
knowing in Western culture are Homer's great
narrative epics the *Iliad* and the *Odyssey.* The
work of Plato, especially *The Republic,* serves as
an exemplum of rational, abstract knowing in
our culture.

Contemporary scholars and writers call the
ways of knowing by different names. Cognitive
psychologist Jerome Bruner labels them the paradigmatic and the narrative; the art educator
Elliot Eisner identifies the literary as part of the
aesthetic. Psychologist Howard Gardner creates
his own category of this kind of knowing: the
personal intelligences, made up of the interpersonal and intrapersonal intelligences.

2 **Two Ways of Knowing: Not Opposed but
Complementary**. Are these two ways of know-

ing—the scientific and literary—mutually exclusive, irreducible one to other? We don't think so. Rather, it makes more sense to think of actual examples of the two modes as being placed along a continuum—or within a mental spectrum—with the purest forms of scientific and literary knowing placed at either end, and with other examples of each lining up somewhere between the two extremes. We know that except for the most unadulterated examples—say imagist poetry at one end and pure mathematical notations at the other—many worthwhile texts exhibit both expository and poetic language.

We argue, furthermore, that if we continue to think of the two ways of knowing as being mutually exclusive—as one versus the other—then do we not set up the modes as antagonistic? Is it not more accurate to think of them as simply two arbitrary ways of knowing that we all should be aware of and that we all should learn to read and write? If we are aware of only one to the exclusion of the other, are we not really depriving ourselves of a command of the widest range of potential language ability and thus of a full mental and emotional life?

Glossary

explication de texte—The French term for what is known in English as "close reading." A method of literary criticism in which the interrelated details of a written work are examined and analyzed in an effort to understand its structure and discover an inherent meaning.

frozen language—Precious literature of a culture the people will not let die, such as Cervantes' *Don Quixote*, Shakespeare's plays, and Lincoln's "Second Inaugural Address," which is literally carved in stone. Term coined by Martin Joos in his little book, *The Five Clocks*.

Multiple Intelligences—Theory proposed by Howard Gardner in his 1985 book, *Frames of Mind: The Theory of Multiple Intelligences*, which are the following: linguistic, musical, logico-mathematical, spatial, bodily kinesthetic, and personal intelligences, consisting of the intrapersonal and inter-

personal intelligences. For Gardner, the personal intelligences overarch all the others.

narrative mode of knowing—Telling stories through fiction, poetry, plays, and through oral transmission by elder family members or case histories by patients of physicians and pychiatrists.

New Criticism—A theory of literary criticism with the the chief emphasis on the text, designed to discover the intrinsic meaning of the literary work. The approach focuses on the close examination (close reading) of a text with minimum regard for the biographical or historical circumstances in which it was produced.

Old Criticism—A theory of literary criticism in which the the chief emphasis is on the author's purpose in writing the work, an interest in the mind and personality of the poet, writer of fiction, or playwright.

paradigmatic mode of knowing—A type of knowing also called rational, abstract, scientific, and mathematical, which, according to the cognitive psychologist, Jerome Bruner, who coined the term, is irreducibly opposed to narrative knowing.

Reader Response criticism—A theory of literary criticism in which the chief emphasis is on the reader's personal interpretation of a text. The theory is concerned with the relationship between the text and reader and reader and text, with the stress on the different ways by which a reader participates in reading a text.

CHAPTER FIVE

Literacy for a Diverse Twenty-First Century

Challenges, Conclusions, and Implications

The new man and the new woman will not be constructed in the heads of educators but in a new social practice, which will take the place of the old that has proven itself incapable of creating new persons . . .

(Freire, 1978, 71)

When we began this book, we set out to define, explore, explain, and discuss many issues around the topic of literacy. Thus, in Chapter One, "Introduction: Rationales, Definitions, and New Directions," we reviewed the major definitions of literacy, the reasons for literacy, as well as introduced some of the central challenges and debates surrounding literacy and literacy acquisition both in the United States and worldwide today. In Chapter Two, "The Foundations of Literacy and Its Consequences," we presented essential information on speaking and writing, as well as exploring the historical perspective of how reading and writing developed in its present form(s). In Chapter Three, "How We Learned to Read," we highlighted the necessary steps one must take in being successful in everyday reading tasks, while discussing

how reading evolved and changed as a consequence of how text itself was represented in written form. And with Chapter Four, "Two Modes of Knowing," we turned toward a discussion of the birth of prose in Western thought as well as an explanation of how we take on the task of reading different kinds of text. In this concluding chapter, we address some of the most timely issues in literacy education today, including those that are crucial in helping us understand the very real concerns, challenges, and debates on literacy in twenty-first century America and beyond.

The Great Literacy Education Debate

Say the word 'literacy' today among educators and other "experts" in the field, and you will undoubtedly hear about some of the major topics and issues we have presented in this primer, including the "characteristics of speech," "how we first [learn to] read," and "how the alphabet works." Say the word "literacy," however, among laypersons in today's society, and you will have undoubtedly helped to stir a pot full of controversy. You may hear comments like, "Why can't urban African Americans and immigrants learn to read?" or "**Phonics** is the best way for children to learn their letters," and "Gosh, the results of the state exams on reading really show teachers aren't doing their jobs!" Unfortunately, it seems in many cases that the sentiments our grandparents heard at the turn of the twentieth century mirror those heard today at the turn of the twenty-first. As immigrants continue to come to the United States at unprecedented rates, discrimination, fear, hatred, and a strong belief that *everyone else* knows best how to learn (and how to teach), reading and writing, the issue of literacy education brings with it questions like "whose literacy?" and "at what cost?"

No matter how similar these sentiments may be, however, there are striking differences in the expectations we in the twenty-first century have of, and for, a literate, and hence, educated populace. Unlike the 1900s, where many unskilled jobs often didn't

phonics

Using sound/symbol correspondence to "sound out" a word.

even require a grade school education, today's society demands that schools train students for a more highly advanced work-world. It is a world in which, in order to compete and be successful, they must be fully literate in a technological, print-and-symbol-oriented culture—a feat often only accomplished with a graduate degree in hand. This is no small task, especially as classrooms in the United States continue to become more diverse, reflecting cultural and learning-style differences, as well as differences in orientations to language and print that are markedly different from Western traditions (e.g., Arabic is written from right to left, from bottom to top, in a different alphabetic system). Combined with increasing pressure on state and local governments to perform to certain **benchmarks** set by policy boards, often out of touch with the reality of today's classrooms, those responsible for literacy education find it to be a formidable task indeed.

In this chapter, we first define and describe who today's diverse learners are. Second, we review the major theories of second language and literacy acquisition (i.e., reading and writing) among diverse learners. Third, we list five assumptions crucial to an understanding of the theoretical premises underlying literacy and diverse learners. Next we situate the entire notion of "becoming literate" within Street's (1995b) ideological model of "**schooled**" versus "**local literacies**," as we offer ideas on how to balance "schooled" literacy education with students' own lives and literacies within a context of increased state and national standardized testing and accountability. Finally, we offer some conclusions and implications on literacy for the twenty-first century including a discussion of ideas such as "literacy across the curriculum," "critical literacy," and Blake's (1997) notion of "**cultural texts**."

benchmarks
Indicators of success in meeting a particular standard.

schooled
literacy most valued in school settings; traditional view of literacy carried out by use of Standard English and the Western canon of literature.

local literacies
Literacy practices embedded in the everyday social and cultural lives of people.

cultural texts
Term that describes a student's written text that reflects his or her life and struggles, challenges, and revealing issues around his or her race, class, gender.

Who are today's diverse learners?

Made up of members of multiple interpretive communities, any group of literacy learners is always "diverse." Here, however, the word "diverse" is used

to refer to students who are culturally and linguistically different from "mainstream" students—including those who come from other countries, those who speak languages other than English at home, and those who by virtue of their socioeconomic status are often deemed "culturally different." These diverse learners' voices have often been silenced (Blake, 1997) and yet, when heard, are vibrant reflections of their distinct experiences and perceptions of the world.

The term "diverse" is often widely used to represent students who have special needs as well as those who may be considered gifted and/or talented. While certainly both of these groups are "diverse" by the very nature of their distinctions, and thereby provide a richness to the **diversity** of our classrooms and of our society at large, here we focus on **diverse learners** as it specifically refers to those whose first language is not English, or **English Language Learners** (**ELLs**). (Please note: Many of these students by virtue of their recent immigrant status to the United States are, therefore, also poor, and thus are doubly-diverse, or "**multiply-marginalized**" as Ayers (1997) has so aptly and eloquently described.)

Diverse learners are the fastest growing group of students in our public school classrooms around the United States. As a result, both urban and rural school districts alike find themselves, under federal law (based on the 1974 Supreme Court case, *Lau v. Nichols*) obligated to set up English as a Second Language (ESL) programs, as numbers of immigrant students continue to add to or fill classrooms. In California, for example, students whose **native language** is a language other than English represent the majority of school-aged children in public schools. In New York City, more than fifty different languages can be heard at any one time throughout this district—the nation's largest—including Bengali, Chinese (Mandarin), French Creole, Russian, Spanish, Vietnamese, and Urdu. One in four children is now raised in a household in this country speaking a

---

diversity

Members of multiple interpretive communities.

---

diverse learners

Students who are culturally and linguistically different from the mainstream; may also include children who are gifted or have special needs.

English Language Learners (ELLs)

Students whose first or native language is not English and are therefore learning English and (American) culture.

---

multiply-marginalized

Term that includes those people who belong to more than one "minority" group (e.g., black and poor).

---

native language

Student's first or home language.

language other than English as his or her first language; there are now four languages in the United States other than English that are regularly spoken by over one million people: Spanish, French, German, and Italian. Soon demographers predict diverse ELLs will become the majority population among school-aged children in, perhaps, less obvious places like Hartford, CT, Rochester, NY, St. Paul, MN, and Fort Wayne, IN. (In fact, Fort Wayne boasts the largest Burmese-speaking population outside of Burma!) And by the mid-twenty-first century, Latinos will constitute close to 40% of the entire public school population.

How Do We Define
English Language Learners (ELLs)?

English language learners can be defined as students whose first language or home language is not English and therefore are learning English as a second language, primarily in school. Additional challenges face these diverse students, however, both in school and out of school. First, ELLs (on average) begin their American school career already significantly behind their U. S. counterparts, often by two to three years. Second, ELLs are not just learning language per se; they are learning to become literate both in language and subject/content areas, such as math and science. Third, ELLs often struggle with issues around identity and self-worth as they work to maintain their home language, customs, and traditions and learn how to adjust to life in American schools and in American culture in general. And finally, diverse learners like ELLs are often discriminated against and assumed to be less intelligent simply because they come from another country and/or speak another language. Unfortunately, in too many classrooms, uncertified or unsympathetic teachers are unable or unwilling to help these students achieve the literacy skills necessary for these diverse learners to be successful both in and out of school. In fact, as Harklau (1999) reports:

[There is often] little support for students' linguis-

tic needs . . . little recognition of fostering of linguistic and ethnic diversity in the school at large and a strong tendency to confound bilingualism with academic deficiency. (56)

ELLs come in many shapes and sizes and can be found in a variety of classrooms and classroom-like settings throughout the United States. These settings can include after-school programs held in synagogues and churches, night classes in migrant camps (Blake, 2004), adolescent programs in jails (Blake, 2004), and weekend tutoring sessions in community outreach centers like the YWCA. There continues to be a huge increase in the numbers of immigrant students—fifteen per hour in New York City alone ("Moving In" [September 17, 2000], *New York Times Magazine,* 1–4)—as well as the variety and mobility of these diverse learners. As a result, most teachers, and especially teachers of literacy, will be asked throughout their careers to teach and work with diverse learners, as they engage in their language and literacy learning.

Where do teachers begin?

Teaching literacy skills to diverse learners is not an easy task, and most teachers report to us that they feel ill-equipped, adding, "We just don't know where to begin!" In our experience as literacy and ESL educators, we believe that one must begin with a basic understanding of how children learn languages as well as how they develop literacy skills in both their native language and in the **target language**, English.

target language
The language that a learner is trying to obtain.

Second Language Acquisition Theories

There are three major theories to explain how a child learns a second language (these theories need to be modified slightly when we are talking about adults, but here we will focus on children from birth to around twelve years of age, or puberty). First, behavioralists believe that language is learned (solely) by imitation and rote memorization. In other words, children are "empty vessels" into which language is

poured. Although behavioralist theory can account for some of a child's early acquisition, it cannot, for example, account for the creative, ingenious words and phrases we hear coming out of children's mouths everyday, like that of five-year-old Brandon Galliher on Thanksgiving Day as he bolted up from the table exclaiming,

Gee Dad, I'm really full of turkey dinner but I think if I stand up for awhile, the food can fall all the way to my toes and then I'll have more room in my stomach!

or phrases like: "longcut" to match "shortcut"; "touchup" instead of "touchdown"; "new lady" as the opposite to "old lady"; "goed" instead of "went"; and so on. The examples are endless, showing that in learning language, children create, construct, and play with language all of the time. In the cases above, no one would ever suspect that a child had heard those words or phrases before—Brandon certainly hadn't heard his dad, Charlie, say anything about food "falling to his toes." If language were only learned by imitation, Brandon would have *had* to have heard those words before, in that order, because he could *only* be mimicking the adults around them. (An additional note on Brandon's exclamation here: children also use language out of *need,* to communicate something; often something they *want.* In this case, Brandon desperately wanted to watch football with his Dad and older brother and also to come back to the table later for a second helping. So to accomplish both these feats, Brandon had to communicate his needs by using language. That is, Brandon at the tender age of five, not only knows how to play with words and phrases, but also how to use language creatively to communicate and get exactly what he wants. **Behavioralism** cannot account for either his "play" or his creativity.)

The "creation" of language is the central focus of the second major theory of second language acquisition: the innatist position. The **innatist theory** (attributed to the seminal work of Noam Chomsky) posits that all human beings are capable of creating an infinite number of phrases in an infi-

behavioralism

Theory that says language is learned primarily by imitation; attributed primarily to Skinner's (1957) work on stimulus and response.

innatist theory

Chomksy's theory (1957) that states that language is innate, hard wired, and creative.

nite number of languages. Chomsky (1957) hypothesizes that humans are "hardwired" with something like a "black box" in our brains that allows us this ability to infinitely create and use language. Around puberty, however, innatists believe that the brain literally hardens or "lateralizes" so that learning a language becomes less natural and fraught with many more challenges.

The third major theory can be called **social interactionism**." A social-interactionist views the communicative give and take of natural conversation between native and non-native speakers as the crucial element of the language acquisition process (Long & Porter, 1985, 207). The focus here is on the social interaction and the subsequent ways in which ELLs adjust their language to be better understood, and the ways in which native English speakers modify their speech to try to make themselves better understood. Meaning is constantly being negotiated and refined; language cannot be learned in isolation and without this dialogic interplay of words, phrases, and certainly of meaning.

None of the above theories, however, highlights the importance of the sociocultural and historical/political contexts in which any language learner is learning a language and hence is developing his or her literacy skills and practices. That is, language is inherently social, cultural, and political, and is situated in historical frameworks that give it status, meaning, and value. By this we mean that language and literacy learning is *never* neutral; which language a student speaks and how that language (and/or home country) is viewed politically, culturally, and even economically may affect the way a student wants to (and is expected to) engage in language and literacy learning. Language is expressed through a wide range of contexts and experiences, contexts that are always present and ever changing. And, importantly, these contexts may differ from our perceptions that **Standard English** is the only acceptable English language dialect in which to communicate, orally and in writing, and to become

social interactionism

Linguistic theory that accounts for the communicative give and take of language-the social aspects.

Standard English

The accepted, grammatically correct, dialect-free form of language spoken by an educated populace.

global society
The larger world community in which we live; connected by technology and common needs/wants.

participants in American schools and society. We must take care to remember that Standard English is but only one way of seeing and expressing oneself in this **global society** in which we all live.

Reading and Second Language

Children who are learning to become literate in English face a dual task: besides the characteristics of written language, they have to learn an unfamiliar language that in large part refers to an unfamiliar cultural background. In fact, the written system from which these students' home language, culture, and identity is embedded may not even be one that uses alphabetic script as represented by the Greek alphabet (refer to Chapter Two for a fuller discussion of the advent of alphabetic script). Students, for example, may read Chinese symbols that represent whole phrases, or read as many do in the Middle East, from bottom to top and from right to left, using an alphabet markedly different from the Greek alphabet.

schema
Background knowledge and experience; term widely used in reading theory.

language transfer
Linguistic theory that describes how language learners extrapolate and/or borrow a rule from the native language to apply in the target language.

decoding
Analyzing parts/distinct sounds of a word to understand meaning.

metacognitive
A person's knowledge about his or her understandings of language and learning; the ability to make one's thinking about this knowledge explicit.

But, this is only part of the challenge. The students' background knowledge, or **schema**, may be so different that **language transfer** in reading can be hindered. It is often not that the students cannot read a particular passage, using **decoding** skills, for example, but it is that they find it difficult to make a connection to the sociocultural context in which all words, and hence, all stories and informational texts are embedded. Further, on a **metacognitive** level, where students are asked to make interpretations of text, often their understandings of particular words, phrases, and whole stories, are predicated upon the sociocultural contexts in which they have developed different interpretations of what we may consider "basic" knowledge. For example, in some countries, *The Three Little Pigs* (Galdone, 1984) is considered vulgar, and thereby, not worthy of an "American" interpretation that may include lessons on greed, friendship, and the value of hard work (i.e., the Protestant work ethic).

More recent research on second language learn-

ing and literacy (Verhoeven, 1999), however, focuses on the "substantial similarities between the strategies employed in first language learning and those in second language learning," and the "home-school" connection between expectations of schooled literacy and various types of literacies and literacy practices in diverse homes around the country. That is, if a diverse student's literacy practices at home match those at school, such as storytime, an abundance of print materials, "book talks" and discussions with children, similar strategies to teach reading, such as simple decoding, **decoding by analogy**, **blending**, and **structural analysis** (such as compounding or working with prefixes and suffixes), can be used fairly effectively. Literacy exposure and development in the first language is generally agreed upon to be a predictor of a diverse student's ability to become a literacy learner in the second language.

Knowing where to begin in teaching reading to diverse learners is predicated on the understandings we have outlined above. These understandings, then, form a crucial theoretical framework or a set of assumptions that are necessary to aid these students' language and literacy growth in positive and successful ways. These are:

decoding by analogy
Decoding an unrecognizable word by thinking of a recognizable word that is like it.

blending
Putting sounds together to form words.

structural analysis
Breaking up an unknown word into its component parts.

Assumption #1:

All students (even students with severe disabilities, such as mental retardation) have the ability to learn and develop with language (although as is the case with a child with a severe disability, language and literacy acquisition may vary). Human beings are unique in this respect.

Assumption #2:

No language is inferior to another and no matter what language the child speaks at home, he or she can develop literacy skills in English given the right tools and encouragement from his or her teacher.

Assumption #3:

All students have a rich background or schema from which to engage in literacy practices. All students have something to say about their lives and experiences, so begin your literacy work with them. Choose books and topics related to their lives. Encourage them to write about their families, or their native lands (see Blake, 1997).

Assumption #4:

Beginning students engage best with literacy activities that are context embedded. Provide your diverse learners with real audiences with hands-on materials that they can hold, taste, and smell. Give them tactile opportunities from which to create.

Assumption #5:

All students like to have fun with literacy. While many states (e.g., New York and California) are implementing state wide assessments and higher standards, take the time to remind children that reading and writing can, and should be, fun!

Standards and Accountability: Role of Schooled versus Local Literacies?

assessment

Ongoing process of evaluation that takes several forms (e.g., tests, observations, portfolios) as a way of measuring student performance and growth.

large-scale/high-stakes testing

Statewide and national standardized tests given to a large population of students and can help determine grade promotion, exit from high school, and/or entrance to college.

As the twenty-first century unfolds, so does the debate on **assessment**, accountability, and standards for both teachers and students in public and private education across the United States. In fact, the terms "**large-scale**" or "**high-stakes**" testing have become synonymous with the notion of "success." Such large-scale assessments literally become a make-or-break situation for students to enter the college of their choice, as well as having important implications for how we, as educators, teach and evaluate all of our students, particularly around their language and literacy growth. Teachers are often compelled to "teach to the test," having to ignore diverse students' real language and literacy needs—and signs of its growth and development—while many of these same students, as a result, suffer seri-

ous consequences that may lead them to "failure" and to dropping out of school altogether (Blake, 1997).

The major challenge to using high-stakes assessment tools as a way to gauge diverse learners' language and literacy development is that these assessments cannot capture their diverse abilities, learning styles, and hence, knowledge in English. Simply put, standardized tests are, according to Fraser, "based on the norms of native English speakers and therefore may be culturally biased." Indeed, "expected prior knowledge" on cultural life in America, *alone,* is enough to become a "deadly pitfall" for all but the most acculturated English language learner (Fraser, 2000, 28).

In other words, these tests cannot measure the real kinds of language and literacy development that are going on in the teachers' classrooms. Large-scale literacy assessments are meant to capture "schooled literacy" (Blake, 2001; Street, 1995b) practices—ability to recall facts and details (of text), ability to use schema to connect to content, ability to reproduce writing in scripted ways without mechanical errors, and of course, the ability to do all of this in Standard American English.

Schooled vs. Local Literacies

technical/rational model
A set of neutral literacy skills most valued by Western society.

This "**technical, rational**" model on which state wide and national assessments are based still prevails throughout our schools today via literacy methodologies that focus on the technical features of language and discrete skills. It remains, therefore, a tool that effectively forces all students (if they are to be successful) to accept a Western, literate ideology.

Interestingly, the academic research on literacy since the 1960s reflects this ideology and can be seen quite clearly in the plethora of work that has examined both the **cognitive predictors** (e.g., socioeconomic class and parents' educational level and income) and the cognitive consequences (e.g., deprivation and correlation between literacy acquisition and dropout rates) of unsuccessful literacy

cognitive predictor
One of several variables used to predict a student's academic and/or school success.

and language development. Language difference, reflected most notably within the literacy practices of students whose predictors did not match white, so-called mainstream middle-class indicators, was recorded as "deficient," and remediation became the standard intervention to align students' literacy practices with the school's literacy practices. Students who did not acquire literacy in a traditional manner that reflected a standard, Western view were labeled, quite simply, "illiterate."

In the late 1970s and early 1980s, however, a grassroots movement of teachers began to flourish. Behind the closed doors of their classrooms, these teachers began implementing curricular and pedagogical change based on what they knew (observationally and intuitively) worked best in helping their students to become literate. The movement itself (alternately called "the **whole language movement**" [Blake, 1989; Goodman, 1986] and the "**integrated language approach**" [Pappas, Keifer, & Levstik, 1990] was solidly grounded in reconstructed theoretical frameworks that afforded (i.e., gave permission to) teachers the opportunities to help students begin to take control of their own literacy learning and to move away from a technical view of literacy.

whole language movement/integrated language approach

Philosophy/approach where teaching and learning are holistic processes where skills are not taught in a preset fashion.

As a result of the whole language movement, both research and practice in holistic and process approaches was prolific throughout the 1980s (Atwell, 1987; Calkins, 1983, 1986; Goodman, 1986; Graves, 1983, 1986), showing quite clearly that students could and did become active participants in their own literacy learning, particularly in writing. Studies of successful classroom models of process writing, for example, highlighted how commonplace it was for students to become motivated to write more, to improve their grammar usage, and to develop a greater sense of community through writing at virtually every grade level. Further, the research on the efficacy of process approaches to literacy among "minority" learners and ELLs, although seemingly slower to develop, did emerge. Notable studies high-

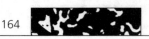

lighted success in general (Dyson & Freedman, 1990; Reyes, 1991); the importance of peer conferencing (Blake, 1992; Gere & Abbott, 1985); the ways in which research in native language literacy could be extrapolated to help explain acquiring literacy in a second language (Hudelson, 1989); and how ELLs, like their first language counterparts—when successful in moving back and forth among the processes of process writing—could produce pieces exhibiting higher **textual readability** and **coherence** (Blake, 1992). Simply put, it was demonstrated that students from all walks of life had more access, and therefore more opportunity, to engage in and become successful in acquiring language and literacy skills.

textual readability

Degree to which a text is understood; level at which a text is understood.

But as much as the process movement moved students' varied learning experiences—and the processes by which they engaged with these learning experiences—to the forefront of our common understanding of what it means to become literate, process approaches also fell short in acknowledging the multiple social, cultural, linguistic, and historical contexts in which students live, and from which they construct their literate selves.

textual coherence

Written text that is consistent and orderly; relates the parts to the whole.

The **New Literacy Studies** of the late 1980s and 1990s, however, put forth the notion of a "plurality" of literacies and was touted by researchers in the field as a reaction to the literacy crisis of the 1980s. Szwed (1981), a pioneer in the field of the New Literacy Studies, claimed that

New Literacy Studies

Term that describes new perspectives on how literacy is used/taught/valued.

> despite the claims of a crisis of "illiteracy," we had not yet conceptualized literacy, nor did we know how literacy or reading and writing were used in social life. (14)

Szwed (1981) was one of the first researchers to look toward literacy in the community, away from the school, finding (among other things) that literacy was not a single entity, but rather that these communities used multiple literacies to negotiate their places in the world. Today, researchers such as Heath (1983), Gee (2000), Street (2001), & Willinsky (1990) focus on how this plurality of literacies is linked to power and power relations throughout the world.

However, it is Street's (1995b) notion of local literacies that truly reconceptualizes our previous work in holistic/process approaches, as it not only builds upon what we knew worked best, but it also extends the perspective of "literacy" to include a strong, ideological base. That is, literacy is an *ideological* practice that is embedded in the everyday social and cultural lives of people (their local literacies) and therefore reflects not a lack of traditional skills, but an addition—a complement to that which is most often taught in schools, and thereby reified by society and its government.

The reification of schooled literacy is, in Street's view (1995b; 2001) done because schooled literacy is seen as something autonomous, universal, and neutral—a "gift" that a government or an educational system bestows upon people in order to lead them to "good social practices" (Street, 2001, 4). And schooled literacy, too, is seen as a civilizing factor—an equalizing factor that ameliorates the lack of social and economic opportunities that poor students would otherwise not have.

In classrooms, then, schooled literacy is realized through the teaching of Standard English (exclusively) and the use of a **Western canon** that not only directs (and/or mandates—see samples of state standards) literary choices, but literacy practices. Indeed, in Kell's (1997) words, schooled literacy can be defined as "sanctioned and thereby framed from within particular textual interpretative processes currently being canonized" (242). While the term local literacies has become a metaphor for agency and voice, schooled literacies remain in the realm of control and power.

The term "local literacies" represents an important ideological and conceptual shift in how the processes of reading and writing are viewed and interpreted, particularly in the schools. We need to reject the notion of an autonomous literacy as the only valid form of literacy and embrace the local literacies of the classroom. This, in turn, helps us to highlight and emphasize the centrality of the social

Western canon

Group of literary works generally accepted as valuable to be taught and learned in school.

nature of literacy in reflecting the multiple ways in which context, culture, and material conditions affect specific literacy practices.

Local Literacies and a Continua of Literacy

Like Street (2001), Hornberger and Skilton-Sylvester (1998) believe that one literacy should not be rejected in lieu of another. (This becomes particularly crucial when talking about access to power and the opportunities for power that learning a schooled literacy affords. See Delpit [1988], Street [2001], and Willis, [1995] for extensive discussions of "minority" students being denied access to the language of power.) In fact, Hornberger posits that we should start from a less binary position where we view literacy and its practices upon a continuum, where, ideally, one can move across at will, choosing which literacy to use at which time. A **continua** of literacy is best described in terms of four frameworks that help define this infinite movement: context, development, content, and media. In Hornberger and Skilton-Sylvester's (1998) view, then, students' development of language and literacy should draw on all points of the continuum, not just those from the more or the less powerful ends.

Specifically, this continuum highlights quite clearly the distinct positions on the continuum that less powerful (local) and more powerful (schooled) literacies fall. In reality, because the more powerful end of the continuum contains points such as "monolingual," "written," "literary," "majority," "decontextualized," and "convergent scripts," becoming literate or biliterate in school and society clearly means focusing one's efforts almost exclusively on these aspects of language and literacy development. On the contrary, focusing on the other end of the continuum, where points such as "oral," "minority," "contextualized," and "divergent scripts" fall means that the act of becoming literate comes at a great risk. At this end, literacy development is relegated to the "personal," to the "oral;" and the "expressive" and, therefore, is not deemed as appropriate in most

continua
View that all literacy learning sits on a continuum that all learners move across.

school settings. While it would be advantageous for all literacy learners to be able to move along this continuum, in reality our schools do not allow this journey. The continuous emphasis on formal "schooled literacy" contexts gives support to the power and privilege schooled literacy enjoys at the expense of local literacies and the contexts in which these literacies are realized.

A Growing International Perspective

As schooled literacy practices are being increasingly canonized around the world (see various accounts on standards and reform in New York State, bilingual education reform in California, literacy reform in South Africa, and national curriculum reform in the United Kingdom and the Czech Republic, for example), fueling a backlash toward alternative perspectives such as Hornberger and Skilton-Sylvester's (1998), challenges are emerging from a body of international and critical literacy scholars whose work is based on theoretical frameworks based in sociolinguistics, ethnography and the ethnography of communication, and the New Literacy Studies.

Led philosophically by Street (1995b) and his work in South Africa, Iran, and the United Kingdom; Hornberger and Skilton-Sylvester (1998) in Cambodia, Puerto Rico, and among indigenous populations in the Andes mountains; and Kell (1997) in post-apartheid South Africa with her work among the settlement populations in Cape Town, these researchers have fashioned an ideological approach to literacy that, as a critical perspective, entirely repositions the notion of what it means to become literate. Rather than solely reflecting the outcomes of schooled literacy, their work emphasizes, quite simply yet eloquently, that throughout the world literacy practices and behaviors are, regardless of the government or schools' efforts, in reality grounded in the everyday lives and experiences of people in their homes and communities.

These scholars write about a crucial need for a synthesis of various notions and definitions of literacy

(some of which we have discussed here and in Chapter One). Specifically, for example, Street (1995b; 2001) puts forth an ideological model that subsumes rather than excludes the work of the rational model; Hornberger and Skilton-Sylvester (1998) envision a continuum where literacy learners are encouraged to journey along all points; and Kell (1997) calls for those in power to understand literacy as a two-way process—one in which those in power provide literacy access to those not in power; those in power learn to "read . . . with [the] understanding of the discourses of those who have been marginalized" (19). In all cases, however, it is understood that both teachers and students need take a critical look at what constitutes literacy, the role of literacy, and the expectations and outcomes (e.g., success) that language and literacy learning can affect.

Using Local Literacies in the Classroom: Becoming Critical/Developing Cultural Texts

The role of literacy educators is undoubtedly a complex one. Arguably, this role has become even more difficult as we are faced with myriad new policies (steeped in public opinion), new standards, statewide and national assessments, greater accountability, and in many cases, fewer resources. And yet, the most compelling challenge comes from within the classrooms; from within ourselves as educators and within the students to whom we are entrusted with our knowledge. We as educators need to begin to examine critically the cultural complexities that surround and infuse everything we teach, especially around the contentious subject of language and literacy learning.

In other words, we educators must interpret and reinterpret perspectives and assumptions around the diverse cultural knowledge and experiences that all children bring to school and, in doing so, find ways in which to extend these conversations into the curriculum (Schubert, 1986).

Giroux (1988) elaborates:

It is imperative for teachers to critically examine the cultural backgrounds and social formations out of which their students produce the categories they use to give meaning to the world. For teachers are not merely dealing with students who have individual interests, they are dealing primarily with individuals whose stories, memories, narratives, and readings of the world are inextricably related to wider social and cultural formations and categories. [The issue] here is not merely one of relevance but one of power. (177)

One powerful way in which to accomplish this in the classroom may be through the use of what Blake (1997) has termed "cultural texts."

When one composes a text, one composes a social self (Bakhtin, 1981, 1986; Dyson, 1992). As students write, they weave stories of their lives and experiences, shaping their texts as they shape their identities. According to Bakhtin, the act of composing a text is always an act of "dialogism." That is, when a writer uses words, she "necessarily engages or responds to past and present discourses," so that each word "smells of the context and contexts in which it has lived its intense social life" (Ewald, 1993, 332).

A cultural text, then, is a text that "smells" of context, of experience, of reality. In the literacy classroom, it is a text that releases scents of gender, race, social class, linguistic heritage, and of community; a text, perhaps, that reflects the particular aspirations, struggles, and realities of these students' literate lives. Cultural texts reflect students' local literacies, as they are the "stuff" of their lives, created and responded to in ways that incorporate the semiotics of a culture (Blake, 1997). Cultural texts are inherently "dialogic" and "answerable" (Bakhtin, 1981, 1986) as multiple voices in a classroom conflict and collide in response to one another. Creating one's own text can be "personally transforming" (Rogers, 1993, 102) as students' writing helps them to connect their lives to other texts in the social world around them, both in and out of school.

Conclusions and Implications:
New Directions for Literacy Learning

The challenges of educating diverse students in twenty-first-century America is much more complex, however, than simply providing a classroom, teachers, and tests. In today's global society, we must also educate society as a whole about diversity, about the potential richness it can add to our lives, about the increased understandings that we can uncover as we listen to different voices, and certainly about our own lives as fellow human beings engaged in literacy and language learning in our own varied, daily interactions with each other and the world.

Literacy learning is a complex act in itself. But it is not so complex, nor so "protected," that it is reserved solely for English speakers or gifted children. Literacy learning, especially when it recognizes the local literacies of diverse learners—students who speak other languages at home, who have special needs, or who come from urban areas where poverty abounds while opportunity falters—should be universally offered and accepted. Literacy should not be seen as a gift from one culture or society to another, not as a "privilege," but as a "right" of all students, an exchange and understanding of many texts, of many voices, of multiple and varied literacies.

In poor communities, in urban black communities, or in rural Latino communities such as jail classrooms and migrant camps in the United States— much like the settlement communities of Cape Town in South Africa (Kell, personal communication, July, 1997)—schooled literacy simply does not "articulate with the existing literacy practices in the community." By its very nature, schooled literacy cannot (and does not, in and of itself) give voice or agency to those less powerful—to the multiply-marginalized youth of any poor urban and rural community throughout the world.

While literacy and social change may go hand-in-hand in post-apartheid South Africa, in the United States literacy is associated with the status quo. In fact, among the multiply-marginalized youth with whom we have worked, literacy often works *against* their success. As they have endured years of racism in our schools while being told they do not have the abilities to become literate in today's technological society, the multiply-marginalized students of the United States often eschew schooled literacy altogether. Fueled in part by a return to teaching and assessment of literacy attainment in discrete and decontextualized ways by states such as New York—which are tied to standards and accountability—advocating for local literacies as measures of success is a major challenge for the future direction of any discussion on language acquisition and literacy today. As radical social change in the United States often seems a vestige of the past, a synthesis of national and international perspectives surrounding literacy and its relationship to economic, social, and political success seems a timely issue for the future. As the United States experiences another huge increase in immigrant populations (resulting in predictions that states such as California will house more nonnative speakers of English than native speakers in the near future) the notion of what it means to become literate will be reshaped and perhaps redefined by these new majorities. And these literacies will indeed be shaped by the daily lives of these people in their homes and in their communities, reflected, perhaps, in the cultural texts that these students create in classrooms across the country and around the world.

Glossary

assessment—An ongoing process of evaluation that takes several forms (e.g., tests, observations, portfolios) as a way of measuring student performance and growth.

large-scale/high-stakes testing—Statewide and national standardized tests that are given to a large population of students and can help determine grade promotion, exit from high school, and/or entrance to college.

benchmarks—Indicators of success in meeting a particular standard.

cognitive predictor—One of several (e.g., environment, social class) variables used to predict a student's academic and/or school success.

cultural texts—Blake's (1995) term that describes a student's written text that reflects his or her life—his or her struggles, challenges—revealing issues around his or her race, class, gender.

diversity—Members of multiple interpretive communities.

diverse learners—Students who are culturally and linguistically different from the mainstream. May also include children who are gifted and those who have special needs.

English Language Learners (ELLs)—Students whose first or native language is not English and are therefore learning English and (American) culture.

global society—The larger world community in which we live; connected by technology and common needs/wants.

language transfer—A linguistic theory that describes how language learners extrapolate and/or borrow a rule from the native language to apply in the target language.

literacy—Reading and writing used to transmit information; to interpret, to respond. The expression of human thought.

Literacy as:

autonomous—The prevailing Western view of literacy; a single view.

continua—Hornberger's (1998) view that all literacy learning sits on a continuum that all learners move across.

critical—View that literacy learning as its central focus must take into account gender, race, class, sexual orientation, disability, etc.

ideological—Street's (1995b) term that situates local literacy learning as a complement to schooled literacy; subsumes rather than replaces other forms of literacy.

local—Literacy practices embedded in the everyday social and cultural lives of people.

multiple—The many and varied forms/expressions of literacy.

rational/technical—A set of neutral literacy skills most valued by Western society.

schooled—Literacy most valued in school settings; traditional view of literacy carried out by use of Standard English and the Western canon of literature.

metacognitive—A person's knowledge about his or her understandings of language and learning; the ability to make one's thinking about this knowledge explicit.

multiply-marginalized—Ayers' (1997) term that includes those people who belong to more than one "minority" group (e.g., black and poor).

native language—Student's first or home language.

New Literacy Studies—Term first coined by Willinsky (1990) that describes new perspectives on how literacy is used/taught/valued.

Reading Strategies

blending—Putting sounds together to form words.

decoding—Analyzing parts/distinct sounds of a word to understand meaning.

decoding by analogy—Decoding an unrecognizable word by thinking of a recognizable word that is like it.

phonics—Using sound/symbol correspondence to "sound out" a word.

structural analysis—Breaking up an unknown word into its component parts.

schema—Background knowledge and experience; term widely used in reading theory.

Second Language Acquisition

Theories of:

behavioralism—Theory that says language is learned primarily by imitation; attributed primarily to Skinner's (1957) work on stimulus and response.

innatist—Chomky's theory (1957) that states that language is innate, hardwired, and creative.

social interactionism—Linguistic theory that accounts for the communicative give and take of language; the social aspects.

Standard English—The accepted grammatically correct, dialect-free form of language spoken by an educated populace.

target language—The language that a learner is trying to obtain.

textual coherence—Written text that is consistent and orderly; relates the parts to the whole.

textual readability—Degree to which a text is understood; level at which a text is understood.

Western canon—Group of literary works generally accepted as valuable to be taught and learned in school.

Whole language movement/Integrated language approach—Grassroots philosophy/approach begun in the 1980s that saw teaching and learning as a holistic process where skills were not taught in a preset fashion.

References and Resources

Print Resources

Atwell, N.M. (1987). *In the middle.* Upper Montclair, NJ: Boynton/Cook.

Ayers, W. (1997). *A kind and just parent: The children of juvenile court.* Boston: Beacon Press.

Bakhtin, M. (1981). *The dialogic imagination.* Austin: University of Texas Press.

Bakhtin, M. (1986). *Speech genres and other late essays.* Austin: University of Texas Press.

Bernard, H.R. (1999). Language and scripts in contact: Historical perspectives. In D.A. Wagner, R.L. Venezky, & B.V. Street (Eds.), *Literacy: An international handbook.* Boulder, CO: Westview Press.

Blake, B.E. (1992). Talk in non-native and native English speakers' peer writing conferences: What's the difference? *Language Arts, 69,* 604–610.

Blake, B.E. (1997). She say, he say: Urban girls write their lives. Albany State University of New York Press.

Blake, B.E. (2001). Using portfolios with English language learners. In J.H. Cohen & R.B. Wiener (Eds.), (2003), *Literacy portfolios: Improving assessment, teaching, and learning.* Upper Saddle River, NJ: Merrill/Prentice Hall.

Blake, B.E. (2004). *A culture of refusal: The lives and literacies of out-of-school adolescents*. New York: Peter Lang.

Blake, R.W. (1978). Composing for the left hand. In P.J. Finn & W.T. Petty (Eds.), *Facilitating language development*. Amherst, NY: State University of New York at Buffalo Press.

Blake, R.W. (1989). *Whole language: Positions and pedagogy*. Urbana, IL: NCTE.

Blake, R.W. (1996). Reader response: Toward an evolving model for teaching literature in the elementary grades. *The Language and Literacy Spectrum*, 6 (Spring), 39–44.

Bobrick, B. (2002). *Wide as the waters. The story of the English Bible and the revolution it inspired*. New York: Penguin Putnam.

Heath, S. B. (1983). *Ways with words*. Cambridge, UK: Cambridge University Press.

Bruner, J. (1985). Narrative and paradigmatic modes of thought. In E. Eisner (Ed.), *Learning and teaching the ways of knowing*. Chicago: University of Chicago Press.

Calkins, L.M. (1983). *Lessons from a child*. Portsmouth, NH: Heinemann.

Calkins, L.M. (1986). *The art of teaching writing*. Portsmouth, NH: Heinemann.

Chomsky, N. (1957). *Syntactic structures*. The Hague, The Netherlands: Mouton.

Coles, R. (1989). *The call of stories: Teaching and the moral imagination*. Boston: Houghton Mifflin.

Damasio, A. (1999). *The feeling of what happens. Body and emotion in the making of consciousness*. Orlando, FL: Harcourt.

Delpit, L.D. (1988). The silenced dialogue: Power and pedagogy in educating other people's children. *Harvard Educational Review*, 58, 84–102.

Dyson, A.H. (1992). Whistle for Willie, lost puppies, and cartoon dogs: The sociocultural dimensions of young children's composing. *Journal of Reading Behavior*, 24, 433–462.

Dyson, A.H. & Freedman, S.W. (1990). *On teaching writing: A review of the literature* (Occasional paper number 20). Berkeley, CA: Center for the Study of Writing.

Eco, U. (1994). *The name of the rose*. San Diego, CA: Harcourt Brace.

Eisenstein, E.L. (1979). *The printing press as an agent of change: Commuications and cultural transformations in early modern Europe*. Cambridge, UK: Cambridge University Press.

Eisenstein, E.L. (1983). *The printing revolution in early modern Europe*. Cambridge, UK: Cambridge University Press.

Eisner, E. (1958). Aesthetic modes of knowing. In E. Eisner (Ed.), *Learning and teaching the ways of knowing*. Chicago: University of Chicago Press.

Ewald, H.R. (1993). Waiting for answerability: Bakhtin and composition studies. *College Composition and Communication, 44*, 331–348.

Fagles, R. (1990). Translator's preface." Homer. *The Illiad*. New York: Penguin Books.

Finley, M.T. (1972). "Introduction." Thucydides. *History of the Peloponnesian War*. New York: Penguin Books.

Fraser, K. (2000, Spring). "The assessment of students with disabilities and students with limited English proficiency: A reflection of what people want out of tests. *The State Education Standard, 27–30*.

Freire, P. (1978). *Pedagogy in process: The letters to Guinea-Bissau*. New York: Continuum.

Galdone, P. (1984). *The three little pigs*. New York: Clarion.

Gall, C. (2002, September 23). Long in the dark, Afghan women say to read is finally to see. *New York Times*, 1, 20.

Gardner, H. (1985). *Frames of mind: The theory of multiple intelligences*. New York: Basic Books.

Gardner, H. (1999). *Intelligence reframed: Multiple intelligences for the 21st century*. New York: Basic Books.

Garner, D. (2001, April 15). "The collector: Interview [with Nicholson Baker]. Author of *Double fold: Libraries and the assault on paper. New York Times Book Review*, 9.

Gates, D. (2001, April 15). Paper chase: Nicholson Baker makes a case for saving old books and newspapers. Review of *Double fold: Libraries and the assault on paper* by Nicholson Baker. *New York Times Book Review*, 8.

Gee, J.P. (2000). New people in new worlds: Networks, the new capitalism, and schools. In B. Cope & M. Kalantzis (Eds.), *Multiliteracies: Literacy learning and design of social futures*. London: Routledge.

Gere, A.R. & Abbott, R.D. (1985). Talking about writing: The language of writing groups. *Research in the Teaching of English, 19*, 362–381.

Giroux, H.A. (1988). *Teachers as intellectuals: Toward a critical pedagogy of learning*. Granby, MA: Bergin & Garvey.

Goodman, K. (1986). *What's whole about whole language?* Portsmouth, NH: Heinemann.

Goody, J. (1968). The consequences of literacy. In J. Goody (Ed.), *Literacy in traditional societies*. Cambridge, UK: Cambridge University Press.

Goody, J. (1986). *The logic of writing and the organization of society.* Cambridge, UK: Cambridge University Press.

Goody, J. (1999). The implications of literacy. In D.A. Wagner, R.L. Venezky, & B.V. Street (Eds.), *Literacy: An international handbook.* Boulder, CO: Westview Press.

Graves, D.H. (1983). *Writing: Teachers and children at work.* Portsmouth, NH: Heinemann.

Graves, D.H. (1986). What children show us about revision. In R.D. Walshe (Ed.), *Donald Graves in Australia.* Rosebery, NSW, Australia: Bridge Printery.

Harklau, L. (1999). The ESL student learning in secondary school. In C.J. Faltis & P. Wolfe (Eds.), *So much to say: Adolescents, bilingualism, and ESL in the secondary school.* New York: Teachers College Press.

Havelock, E.A. (1963). *A preface to Plato.* Cambridge, MA: Harvard University Press.

Havelock, E.A. (1976). *Origins of Western literacy.* Toronto: The Ontario Institute for Studies in Education.

Heath, S. B. (1983). *Ways with words.* Cambridge, UK: Cambridge University Press.

Hornberger, N.H. & Skilton-Sylvester, E. (1998, April). Revisiting the continua of biliteracy: International and critical perspectives. Paper presented at the Annual Meeting of the American Educational Research Association, San Diego, CA.

Hudelson, S. (1989). *Write on: Children writing in ESL.* Englewood Cliffs, NJ: Prentice Hall.

Joos, M. (1967). *The five clocks.* New York: Harcourt, Brace & World.

Kell, C. (1997). Literacy practices in an informal settlement. In M. Prinsloo & M. Breir (Eds.), *The social uses of literacy: Theory and practice in South Africa.* Philadelphia: John Benjamin Press.

Kilborn, P.T. (2000, July 27). Illiteracy pulls Appalachia back, and efforts to overcome it grow. *New York Times,* A1, A16.

Kitto, H. D. F. (1997). *The Greeks.* New York: Penguin Books.

Knox, B. (1990). "Introduction." Homer. *The Iliad.* Translated by R. Fagles. New York: Penguin Books.

Lee, D. (2003). "Translator's Introduction." Plato. *The republic.* New York: Penguin Books.

Long, M. & Porter, P. (1985). Groupwork, interlanguage talk, and second language acquisition. *TESOL Quarterly,* 19(2), 207–228.

Lord, A. B. (2000). *The singer of tales.* Second Edition. Cambridge, MA: Harvard University Press.

Matthiessen, P. (2000). *Tigers in the snow.* New York: Farrar, Straus and Giroux.

Mayor, F. (1999). Forward. In D.A. Wagner, R.L. Venezky, & B.V. Street (Eds.), *Literacy: An international handbook.* Boulder, CO: Westview Press.

McGrath, A. (2002). *In the beginning. The story of the King James Bible and how it changed a nation, a language, and a culture.* New York: Anchor Books, Random House.

Mendelsohn, D. (2004). "Theatre at war. Why the battles of ancient Athens still rage." *The New Yorker.* January 12, 2004, 79–94.

Moving In. (2000, September 17). *New York Times Magazine,* 14.

Olson, D.R. (1991). Literacy and objectivity: The rise of modern science. In D.R. Olson & N. Torrance (Eds.), *Literacy and orality.* Cambridge, UK: Cambridge University Press.

Olson, D.R. (1994). *The world on paper. The conceptual and cognitive implications of writing and reading.* New York: Cambridge University Press.

Olson, D.R. (1999). Literacy and language development. In D.A. Wagner, R.L. Venezky, & B.V. Street (Eds.), *Literacy: An international handbook.* Boulder, CO: Westview Press.

Pappas, C., Keifer, B., & Levstik, L. (1995). *An integrated language perspective in the elementary school.* White Plains, NY: Longman.

Plato. (2003). The *republic.* Translated by Desmond Lee, Second Edition. New York: Penguin Books.

Reyes, M. (1991). A process approach to literacy instruction for Spanish-speaking students: In search of a best-fit. In E.H. Hiebert (Ed.), *Literacy for a diverse society: Perspectives, practices, and policies.* New York: Teachers College Press.

Rogers, A. (1993). Voice, play, and a practice or ordinary courage in girls' and women's lives. *Harvard Educational Review,* 63, 265–295.

Rohde, D. (2001, October 3). Education offers women in northern Afghanistan a ray of hope. *New York Times,* B6.

Saenger, P. (1997). *Space between words: The origins of silent reading.* Stanford, CA: Stanford University Press.

Saenger, P. (1999). The history of reading. In D.A. Wagner, R.L. Venezky, & B.V. Street (Eds.), *Literacy: An international handbook.* Boulder, CO: Westview Press.

Schaller, G.C. (1998). Tiger. In *The World Book Encyclopedia.* T. Vol. 19. Chicago: World Book.

Schmetzeer, U. (2000, February 20). Literacy empowers, gives hope to Indian women. *Rochester, NY, Democrat and Chronicle* (reprinted from *Chicago Tribune*), 14A.

Schubert, W.H. (1986). *Curriculum: Perspective, paradigm, and possibility.* New York: Macmillan.

Sella, M. (2001, December 6). The crawl. The year in ideas: A to Z. *New York Times Magazine,* 66.

Spurgeon, C.F.E. (1952). *Shakespeare's imagery and what it tells us.* Cambridge, UK: The University Press.

Street, B.V. (1995a). *Critical approaches in development, ethnography, and education.* New York: Longman.

Street, B.V. (1995b). *Social literacies: Critical approaches to literacy in development, ethnography, and education.* London: Longman.

Street, B.V. (1999). The meanings of literacy. In D.A. Wagner, R.L. Venezky, & B.V. Street (Eds.), *Literacy: An international handbook.* Boulder, CO: Westview Press.

Street, B.V. (Ed.). (2001). *Literacy and development: Ethnographic perspectives.* London: Routledge.

Szwed, J.F. (1981). The ethnography of literacy. In Whiteman (Ed.), *Writing: The nature, development, and teaching of written communication, part I.* Hillsdale, NJ: Lawrence Erlbaum.

Thomas, R. (1992). *Literacy and orality in ancient Greece.* Cambridge, UK: Cambridge University Press.

Thucydides. (1972). *History of the Peloponnesian war.* Translated by R. Warner. New York: Penguin.

Venezky, R.L. (1990). *Toward defining literacy.* Newark, DE: International Reading Association.

Verhoeven, L. (1999). Second language reading. In D.A. Wagner, R.L. Venezky, & B.V. Street (Eds.), *Literacy: An international handbook.* Boulder, CO: Westview Press.

Wagner, D.A. (1999). Rationales, debates, and new directions: An introduction. In D.A. Wagner, R.L. Venezky, & B.V. Street (Eds.), *Literacy: An international handbook.* Boulder, CO: Westview Press.

Waldman, A. (2003, November 15). India's poorest bet precious sums on private schools. *New York Times,* A1, A5.

Willinsky, J. (1990). *The new literacy: Redefining reading and writing in the schools.* New York: Routledge.

Willis, A.I. (1995). Reading the world of school literacy: Contexualizing the experience of a young African-American male. *Harvard Educational Review,* 65(1), 30–49.

Winchester, S. (2001, April 8). Where is it written? Right here. Review of *Wide as the waters* by Benson Bobrick and *In the beginning* by Alister McGrath. *New York Times Book Review,* 8.

Additional Resources

The additional works listed in this chapter are divided into three categories. The first section entitled "Further Suggested Readings" includes text references that are both popular and scholarly in nature and include conference presentations and other studies that deal with the topic of literacy in its broadest sense. The list is not annotated, but it is important to note that many of these particular resources deal with the controversial nature of literacy, including literacy and politics, literacy and ethnicity/race, and notions of "whose literacy?" They are included here to present a balanced portrait of the nature of literacy education today.

The second section of the chapter, "Web Resources," contains nonprint resources such as websites and Internet research sites that include lesson plans, teaching resources, and research, including articles from the ERIC database and various professional organizations and publishers.

Finally, the third section of the chapter, "Organizations, Foundations, and Educational Associations," provides brief information on some of the organizations, foundations, and educational associations that have a direct interest in literacy and literacy learning as a broad category. Because literacy is currently a major concern to national and state governments, general information on literacy, including state standards and assessments, can also be found at each of the fifty states' education websites. Check links through your state's government or education web pages.

Further Suggested Readings

Bhola, H.S. (1984). *Campaigning for literacy.* Paris: UNESCO.

Blake, B.E. (1995). Broken silences: Writing and the construction of 'cultural texts' by urban, pre-adolescent girls. *Journal of Educational Thought, 29,* 165–180.

Blake, B.E. (1995). Doing number 5: From process to cultural texts in an urban writing classroom. *Language Arts, 72,* 396–404.

Blake, B.E. (1998). 'Critical' reader response in an urban classroom: Creating cultural texts to engage diverse readers. *Theory Into Practice, 37*(3), 238–243.

Blake, B.E. (2001). Fruit of the devil: Writing and English language learners. *Language Arts, 78*(5), 435–441.

Blake, B.E. & Blake, R.W. (2002). *Literacy and learning: A reference handbook.* Santa Barbara, CA: ABC-CLIO.

Brandt, D. (1990). *Literacy as involvement: The acts of writers, readers, and texts.* Carbondale: Southern Illinois University Press.

Cohen, J.H. & Wiener, R.B. (2003). *Literacy portfolios: Improving assessment, teaching, and learning.* Upper Saddle River, NJ: Merrill/Prentice Hall.

Freire, P. (1987). *Literacy: Reading the word and the world.* Boston: Bergin & Garvey.

Gunning, T.G. (2003). *Building literacy in the content areas*. Boston: Allyn & Bacon.

Hoggart, R. (1957). *The uses of literacy*. London: Penguin.

Hull, G. & Schultz, K. (Eds.). (2002). *School's out: Bridging out-of-school literacies with classroom practice*. New York: Teachers College Press.

McLaren, P. (1988). Culture or canon? Critical pedagogy and the politics of literacy. *Harvard Educational Review, 58*.

Mercer, N. (Ed.). (1988). *Language and literacy from an educational perspective*. Milton Keynes, UK: Open University Press.

Olson, D., Torrance, N., & Hildyard, A. (Eds.). *Literacy, language and learning: The nature and consequences of reading and writing*. Cambridge, UK: Cambridge University Press.

Ong, W. (1982). *Orality and literacy*. London: Methuen.

Ornstein, A.C. (2003). *Pushing the envelope: Critical issues in education*. Upper Saddle River, NJ: Pearson.

Rodby, J. (1992). *Appropriating literacy: Writing and reading in English as a second language*. Portsmouth, NH: Heinemann.

Roe, B.D., Stoodt-Hill, B.D., & Burns, P.C. (2004). *Secondary school literacy instruction: The content areas*. Boston: Houghton Mifflin.

Scollon, R. & Scollon, S. (1981). *Narrative, literacy, and face in interethnic communication*. Norwood, NJ: Ablex.

Scribner, S. & Cole, M. (1981). *The psychology of literacy*. Cambridge, MA: Harvard University Press.

Sinatra, R. (2003). *Word recognition and vocabulary: Understanding strategies for literacy success*. Norwood, MA: Christopher-Gordon.

Smith, F. (1984). *Joining the literacy club*. Victoria, Alberta: ABEL Press.

Street, B. (1984). *Literacy in theory and practice*. Cambridge, UK: Cambridge University Press.

Street, B. (Ed.). (1993). *Cross-cultural approaches to literacy*. Cambridge, UK: Cambridge University Press.

Stuckey, E. (1991). *The violence of literacy*. Portsmouth, NH: Boynton/Cook.

Wagner, D. (1987). *The future of literacy in a changing world*. Oxford: Pergamon Press.

Weinstein, G. (1984). Literacy and second language acquisition: Issues and perspectives. *TESOL Quarterly, 18*, 471–484.

Web Resources

General Interest

Center for Applied Linguistics
http://www.cal.org
Dedicated to "improving communication through better understanding of language and culture," this center's comprehensive site
features research and teaching materials for ESL, foreign languages, and linguistics.

Children's Book Council's Teacher and Librarian Page
http://www.cbcbooks.org/
Offers links to a variety of bibliographies, brochures, and hand-
outs geared toward teachers and librarians.

Children's Literacy Development with Suggestions for Parental
Involvement
http://eric.indiana.edu/www.indexdb.html
An ERIC Reading, English, and Communication digest, a project
of the U.S. Department of Education with funding from the
Library of Education.

Choose the Right Book for Kids
http://www.members.aol.com/ivonavon/booklis.html
A set of links to bibiolographies of the "best" books for children.

ESL Magazine Online
http://www.eslmag.com
This site features abstracts of articles from the print magazine for
English as a Second Language (ESL) educators. Helpful ESL links
are included.

George Suttle's "Reading and Language Arts Resources on the Internet"
http://GeorgeSuttle.com/presentations/MSRC/index.shtml
This fully annotated website, compiled and maintained by George
Suttle, includes links to many websites that he encourages for use
for educational purposes. He welcomes any comments, suggestions,
and questions, and can be reached directly at George@GeorgeSuttle.
com.

Family Education
http://www.familyeducation.com/home/
This site is an engaging, interactive site that provides an information center for parents of K–12 students. It includes articles, tips,
and downloads in addition to an "ask the experts" for help and
support.

Let's Read!
> http://www.ed.gov/pubs/parents/LearnPtnrs/read.html
> Advice from the U.S. Department of Education for parents on how
> to read to their children. Includes reading activities and resources
> for beginning to advanced young readers.

Multicultural Resources for Children
> http://falcon.jmu.edu/~ramseyil/multipub.html
> Offers a series of bibliographies on books about different ethnic
> and cultural groups as well as links to other sites.

National Clearinghouse for English Language Acquisition
> http://www.ncela.gwu.edu
> This site offers technical assistance on important issues related to
> linguistically and culturally diverse students. Users will find links
> to government and professional sites.

Ten Ways to Help Your Children Become Lifelong Readers
> http://www.naeyc.org/
> A handy set of suggestions and ideas—ideal for sharing with
> parents.

United States Department of Education
> http://www.ed.gov/pubs/parents
> The US Department of Education's website provides free, high-
> quality materials that help promote parent involvement in their
> children's education. Publications devoted to "Reading
> Improvement" give parents specific ways to help their children to
> become successful in their literacy learning.

What Do You Know About Reading to Your Child?
> http://www.babycenter.com/calculator/6512.html/
> A ten-question self-quiz to "test" parents on how much they
> know about the power of reading to children. Includes related top-
> ics, including tips on writing.

Lesson Plans and Teaching Resources

Ask ERIC Lesson Plans
> http://ericir.syr.edu/Virtual/Lessons
> A wealth of information designed for the literacy educator and
> beyond.

Classroom Material
> http://www.sonoma.edu/Cthink/K12/k12class/trc.nclk
> The Center for Critical Thinking has compiled a large amount of
> information, including instructional guides and lesson plans to
> help educators.

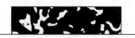

ESL/Bilingual/Foreign Language Lesson Plans and Resources
http://www.csun.edu/~hcedu013/eslindex.html
Created by a teacher educator at California State University, this site provides many helpful links to lesson plans, resources, and standards.

Enhancing Student Literacy in Secondary Schools
http://www.bced.gov.bc.ca/irp/ela1112tpc/toc.html
An in-service resource guide provided by the Curriculum and Resources branch of the British Columbia Ministry of Education.

ESL Lounge
http://www.esl-lounge.com
This excellent teachers' website is loaded with lesson plans, worksheets, teaching tips, printable board games, and reviews of notable ESL books.

Exemplary Sample Lesson Plans
http://eric.indiana.edu/www/indexbs.html
Links to sample lesson plans found in books available from the ERIC bookstore.

Homework Central
http://www.homeworkcentral.com
Students will benefit from accessing the study games and test preparation, while teachers will appreciate the over 14,000 searchable lesson plans that are available.

Kathy Schrock's Guide for Educators
http://discoveryschool.com/schrockguide/world/worldrw.html
Links are included to many sites, including those for ESL and foreign language teachers. Several online resources are listed for both teachers and students.

Literacy Research

Center for the Improvement of Early Reading Achievement
http://www.ciera.org/
Most of the Center's publications are for sale, but the Center does provide some free research articles.

ERIC Clearinghouse on Reading, English, and Communication
http://eric.indiana.edu/www.indexdb.html
Almost no one has time to keep abreast of all the research being done in literacy. This digest provides summaries published by the ERIC Clearinghouse, offering both general awareness and guides to further research.

Learning to Read: Resources for Language Arts and Reading Research
http://www.toread.com
The purpose of this website is to help improve the quality of reading instruction through the study of the reading process and teaching techniques.

1–2-3 Reading Road
http://www.thinkquest.org
Developed as a ThinkQuest project, this website provides a multimedia experience to enable young children to practice the basic skills necessary for reading success. The site supports parents and teachers by providing additional teaching methods, games, and activities.

The Politics of Reading Research and Practice
http://ed-web3.educ.msu.edu/pearson/ppt/polit/index.htm
A research paper by renowned literacy scholar P. David Pearson, formerly of the Center for the Study of Professional Development at Michigan State University.

Preventing Reading Difficulties in Young Children
http://www.nap.edu/readingroom/books/prdyc/
This highly acclaimed study synthesizes the research on early reading development and makes practical recommendations.

Reading OnLine: An Electronic Journal of the International Reading Association
http://www.readingonline.org/
This peer-reviewed online journal for literacy educators includes full-text research articles and offers online forums for readers to react and interact.

Stony Brook Reading and Language Project
http://www.read+lang.sbs.sunysb.edu/
Grover Whitehust provides this introductory page for the SUNY Stony Brook project. From the introduction, one can proceed to pages on the project or to a list of papers and publications.

Teaching Ideas: Reading
http://www.ncte.org/teach/read.html
The National Council of Teachers of English website contains a variety of short essays and excerpts from its publications.

Organizations, Foundations, and Educational Associations

American Federation of Teachers (AFT)
555 New Jersey Ave., NW
Washington, DC 20001

(202) 879–4400

http://www.aft.org

One of the largest teachers' unions in the United States, the AFT
is a good source for information on a broad array of topics, including guidelines and expectations for teachers of literacy and related
topics.

American Literacy Council

1201 15th Street, NW

Suite 420

Washington, DC 20005

(202) 955–6183

Fax: (202) 955–5492

http://www.barbarabushfoundation.com

The foundation is dedicated to establishing literacy as a value in
every family in America. It provides publications for parents about
how to foster literacy and literacy practices with their children.

Beginning with Books

5920 Kirkwood St.

Pittsburgh, PA 15206

(412) 361–8560

http://www.beginningwithbooks.org

Beginning with Books focuses on increasing the number of children who are lifelong readers through programs for low-income
families.

BlakeCo International

15 Dunwood Road

Port Washington, NY 11050

Email: adolescentdr@aol.com or bobbillydumpling@ aol.com

This New York City area-based educational consulting group provides consulting, workshops, and advocacy for both public and
private schools and agencies in language and literacy learning, particularly in urban and other "challenged" settings.

BookPALS

www.bookpals.net (This main site will direct you to a list of state-
by-state local sites.)

Ellen Nathan, National Coordinator

Email: Enathan@bookpals.net

PALS is Performing Artists for Literacy in Schools. Professional actors
read aloud to children at public elementary schools, provide
workshops in theatre and art, connect them to literacy activities,
and promote reading and writing. BookPALS also provides recommended reading lists.

California Literacy, Inc.
2028 East Villa St.
Pasadena, CA 91107–2379
(626) 395–9989 or (800) 894-READ
Email: office@caliteracy.org
http://www.caliteracy.org
Founded in 1956, the nation's largest and oldest statewide volunteer literacy organization establishes literacy programs and supports them through tutor training, consulting, and ongoing education. California Literacy is also involved in designing and supporting programs for students with learning disabilities.

Center for the Improvement of Early Reading Achievement (CIERA)
University of Michigan School of Education
Room 1600 SEB
610 University Ave.
Ann Arbor, MI 48109–1259
(734) 647–6940
Fax: (734) 615–4858
http://www.ciera.org/
CIERA is a national center for research on early reading and literacy, supported under the Federal Educational Research and Development Center program. The center provides free research articles as well as for-sale publications on a wide range of literacy topics.

The Children's Book Council
12 West 37th Street, 2nd floor
New York, NY 10018–7480
(212) 966–1990
Fax: (212) 966–2073
http://www.cbcbooks.org
A nonprofit trade association, the Children's Book Council's membership publishes and packages test booklets to measure literacy achievement, as well as promoting the enjoyment of literacy by sponsoring National Children's Book Week and National Children's Poetry Week each year.

Children's Literature for Children
104 Madison Ave.
Peachtree City, GA 30269
http://www.childrensliterature.org/
This nonprofit organization is dedicated to bringing children and books together by implementing and supporting teaching programs in elementary schools serving disadvantaged children as well as providing books and literacy experiences to hospitalized and housebound children.

Coalition for Essential Schools (CES)
    1814 Franklin St.
    Suite 700
    Oakland, CA 94612
    (510) 433–1451
    Fax: (510) 433–1455
    http://www.essentialschools.org
    The CES is a national network of schools and regional offices, as well as a national center where teachers work to perfect their craft of teaching literacy toward the goal of national school reform.

Ezra Jack Keats Foundation
    http://www.ezra-jack-keats.org
    Ezra Jack Keats, a well-known children's author who died in 1983, directed that all royalties from sales of his books be used to support programs focused on literacy and literacy development among children. These programs include storytelling in public libraries and sponsorship of a UNICEF award for best book illustrator.

First Book National Book Bank
    1319 F Street, NW
    Suite 1000
    Washington, DC 20004–1155
    (202) 393–1222
    Email: staff@firstbook.org
    First Book National Book Bank is the first centralized system enabling publishers to donate large quantities of books to the nonprofit sector for distribution to children from low-income families participating in community-wide programs.

International Book Project, Inc.
    Van Meter Building
    1440 Delaware Ave.
    Lexington, KY 40505
    (888) 999-BOOK
    The International Book Project promotes global friendship and world literacy through book distribution projects.

Literacy Volunteers of America
    P.O. Box 6506
    Syracuse, NY 13217
    (315) 472–0001
    Fax: (315) 472–0002
    http://www.literacyvolunteers.org
    This nonprofit educational organization provides training, tech-

nical assistance, and community and program support to literacy programs. Most larger communities have a local branch, and the main website can be searched by town or county to find local branches.

National Institute for Literacy
1775 I Street, NW
Suite 730
Washington, DC 20006
(202) 233–2025
http://www.nifl.gov/
This federal organization strives to ensure that all Americans with literacy needs have access to services that can help them gain the basic skills necessary for success. It shares information about literacy and supports the development of high-quality literacy services.

National Jewish Coalition for Literacy
P.O. Box 202
Accord, MA 02018
(781) 925–9545
http://www.njcl.net
The National Jewish Coalition for Literacy is the Jewish community's vehicle for participation in childhood literacy initiatives. The coalition encourages local participation where literacy efforts are needed.

National Right to Read Foundation (NRRF)
P.O. Box 490
The Plains, VA 20198
http://www.nrrf.org
The goal of the NRRF is to improve literacy nationwide through phonics and good literature instruction.

Read In Foundation
6043 Channel Dr.
Riverbank, CA 96367
(209) 869–3945
http: //www.reading.org
Email: jane@readin.org
The foundation promotes global literacy and the use of telecommunications technology in education. It sponsors an annual project connecting authors and kids through chat rooms with an underlying focus on developing strong reading skills.

Readers & Writers

PEN American Center
568 Broadway
New York, NY 10012–3225
(212) 334–1660
Fax: (212) 334–2181
http://www.pen.org/readers/info/program/html
Readers & Writers uses literature to promote literacy by sending writers and their books to schools, prisons, community groups, and other organizations nationwide.

Reading Is Fundamental (RIF)
1825 Connecticut Ave., NW
Suite 400
Washington, DC 20009
(877) RIF-READ
http://www.rif.org
Founded in 1966, RIF develops and delivers children's and family literacy programs that help prepare children for reading success. In the past, RIF has also donated large quantities of paperback books to schools in need.

Student Coalition for Action in Literacy Education (SCALE)
208 N. Columbia St.
University of North Carolina at Chapel Hill
CB #3505
Chapel Hill, NC 27599
(919) 962–1542
http://www.readwriteact.org
This national organization supports campus-based literacy programs across the country. College students serve as literacy tutors or teachers in their communities. SCALE provides a full range of technical assistance in this endeavor.

Educational Associations

American Educational Research Association (AERA)
1230 17th St., NW
Washington, DC 20036
(202) 223–9485
http://www.AERA.net
AERA promotes educational research and its practical application in schools and other educational settings. It is concerned with the improvement of the educational process and with the literacy process worldwide.

International Reading Association (IRA)
    800 Barksdale Rd.
    P.O. Box 8139
    Newark, DE 19714–8139
    (302) 731–1600
    Fax: (302) 731–1057
    http://www.reading.org/
    IRA promotes literacy worldwide through publications, conferences, community activities, international projects, resources, advocacy, and professional development. Each state has an IRA affiliate.

National Council of Teachers of English (NCTE)
    1111 W. Kenyon Rd.
    Urbana, IL 61801–1096
    (800) 369–6283
    Fax: (217) 328–9645
    http://www.ncte.org/
    Since 1911, NCTE has provided a forum for educators to deal with all issues related to the development and improvement of the teaching of English, language arts, and literacy. Each state has an NCTE affiliate. Some of the larger NCTE affiliates are:

California Association of Teachers of English (CATE)
    http://www.cateweb.org

Florida Council of Teachers of English
    http://www.fcte.org

Illinois Council of Teachers of English
    http://www4.district125.k12.il.us/CA/IATEpages/

Maryland Council of Teachers of English Language Arts (MCTELA)
    http://www.mctela.org

New England Association of Teachers of English (NEATE)
    http://www.neate.org

The New York State English Council (NYSEC)
    http://www.nysecteach.org

Teachers of English to Speakers of Other Languages (TESOL)
    700 S. Washington St.
    Suite 200
    Alexandria, VA 22314
    (703) 836–0774
    Email: info@tesol.org
    http://www.tesol.org

This organization is dedicated to the education of English language learners in the United States and worldwide. Its goal is to foster effective communication and literacy skills in diverse settings while respecting individual language rights. Most states have local TESOL affiliates.

Peter Lang
PRIMERS
in Education

Peter Lang Primers are designed to provide a brief and concise introduction or supplement to specific topics in education. Although sophisticated in content, these primers are written in an accessible style, making them perfect for undergraduate and graduate classroom use. Each volume includes a glossary of key terms and a References and Resources section.

Other published and forthcoming volumes cover such topics as:

- Standards
- Popular Culture
- Critical Pedagogy
- Literacy
- Higher Education
- John Dewey
- Feminist Theory and Education
- Studying Urban Youth Culture
- Multiculturalism through Postformalism
- Creative Problem Solving
- Teaching the Holocaust
- Piaget and Education
- Deleuze and Education
- Foucault and Education

Look for more Peter Lang Primers to be published soon. To order other volumes, please contact our Customer Service Department:

  800-770-LANG (within the US)
  212-647-7706 (outside the US)
  212-647-7707 (fax)

To find out more about this and other Peter Lang book series, or to browse a full list of education titles, please visit our website:
  www.peterlangusa.com